I0416408

FREIDA BAILEY

How To Invest For Your Future

Your Blueprint to Financial Triumph and Unparalleled Wealth

Copyright © 2024 by Freida Bailey

All rights reserved. No part of this publication may be reproduced, stored or transmitted in any form or by any means, electronic, mechanical, photocopying, recording, scanning, or otherwise without written permission from the publisher. It is illegal to copy this book, post it to a website, or distribute it by any other means without permission.

Freida Bailey asserts the moral right to be identified as the author of this work.

First edition

This book was professionally typeset on Reedsy.
Find out more at reedsy.com

Contents

1

Introduction

I n the complex fabric of life, having enough money is essential to have possibilities and fulfillment in the future. Greetings and welcome to *"How to Invest for Your Future,"* an extensive manual created to assist you in achieving financial security.

Why Make An Investment? The solution to this question, which reverberates across the personal financial industry, is interwoven throughout the pages of this book. A deep understanding exists underneath the complexities of markets and the appeal of returns: the ability of strategic investment to turn dreams into concrete reality.

Embark on an extraordinary adventure across the worlds of real estate, equities, bonds, and strategic planning. This book isn't just about making money; it's also about creating a road plan that fits your goals and making sure that your tomorrow is meaningful. You can be confident that this isn't simply another investment guide as we explore practical solutions and manage risk. It is your travel buddy, providing financial guidance, practical examples, and a compass.

Get ready for a radical change in the way you think about investing. This is about the story of your life that these investments may write, not just about figures on a balance sheet. For those who are new to investing or experienced, this book serves as a valuable resource for creating a rich and satisfying future.This is where the trip starts. Welcome to a future in which your financial legacy is being painted by strategic investments like a masterpiece.

Overview of the importance of investing

Investing is one thread that stands out as a beacon of financial empowerment in the complex fabric of personal finance. Investing and letting your money grow is not just a smart financial move; it's essential to ensuring a prosperous future.

Knowing the Fundamentals:

Investing is, in its simplest form, the conscious allocation of resources with the long-term goal of producing a profit. This can be in the form of conventional stocks and bonds, real estate, mutual funds, and other financial products, among other things. In contrast to saving, which usually entails storing money, investing is using your money to make investments in financial markets.

Wealth Building and Compounding:

The ability of investing to accumulate money over time is one of the main factors making it so important. Invested money can yield returns through the power of compounding, and those returns can yield yet more returns. Your initial investment will grow at a faster rate thanks to this compounding effect.

Imagine the following situation: you invest a certain amount of money and receive a return on it. You reinvest those earnings rather than taking them out, which makes it possible for your investment to yield returns on both the initial investment and the cumulative gains. This compounding effect has the potential to produce exponential growth over time, building a sizeable financial nest egg.

Defying Inflation:

The progressive rise in prices of goods and services over time, known as inflation, reduces the purchasing power of money. Money left in low-interest savings accounts may find it difficult to keep up with inflation. However, investing has the potential to generate returns that exceed inflation, protecting and even increasing your spending power.

Reaching Financial Objectives:

Investing is a dynamic instrument that can be customized to help individuals reach their specific financial goals rather than a one-size-fits-all endeavor. Whether the goal is to finance a child's education, save for a dream home, or ensure a happy retirement, a well-designed investing strategy can help make these goals a reality faster.

Security for Retirement:

Investing to ensure a pleasant retirement is maybe one of the best arguments. Retirement funding is becoming more and more the responsibility of the individual as traditional pension schemes grow less prevalent. Putting money into retirement accounts, like 401(k)s or IRAs, enables people to take advantage of compound interest over many years, creating a sizable retirement fund.

Both Risk Management and Diversification:

While there are hazards associated with investing, wise investors use ways to reduce these risks. Investing across a variety of asset types, or diversification, helps lessen the effects of market volatility. By keeping your money spread out among multiple accounts, you build a more stable portfolio that can withstand fluctuations in the market.

Knowledge of finance and making well-informed decisions:

Investing requires a certain level of financial understanding. Individuals get better at making wise financial decisions as they gain knowledge about various investment possibilities, risk profiles, and market dynamics. This ongoing learning process improves people's financial literacy while also giving them the confidence to confidently traverse the complicated world of investments.

Job Creation and Economic Growth:

Looking broader than personal experiences, investment is essential to promoting economic expansion. Individuals contribute to capital development when they invest in enterprises, whether directly or through stocks. This money then stimulates growth, innovation, and the creation of jobs, resulting in a positive feedback cycle that helps investors and the economy as a whole.

Setting financial goals

Setting and achieving financial goals is essential to being financially successful, whether one's goals are to become financially independent, save for a dream home, or guarantee a happy retirement

The Power of Intention:

Fundamentally, financial goal-setting is defining specific targets for one's financial future. It is more than just wishful thinking; it offers a road map that influences investment choices, savings plans, and spending patterns. When people set deliberate financial objectives, they give their financial journey a purpose and transform their aspirations into tangible strategies.

Clarity in Vision:

Establishing financial objectives helps to clear up the frequently hazy areas of personal finance. It forces people to pose important questions to themselves, like: What are my financial goals? When do I hope to accomplish it? What is the amount I require? These questions assist people in better understanding their beliefs and priorities in addition to giving them a feeling of direction.

Short-Term and Long-Term Goals:

Financial objectives come in a variety of forms, from immediate desires to long-term plans. A few examples of short-term objectives are setting up an emergency fund, paying off high-interest debt, and setting aside money for a trip. On the other hand, long-term objectives frequently center on significant life milestones like retirement preparation, home ownership, and educational costs. For a financial strategy to be holistic, these two groups must be balanced.

Motivation and Discipline:

Having financial objectives is a great way to stay motivated. People are more likely to maintain discipline and focus in their financial endeavors when they have a clear understanding of their goals. Saving and investing become deliberate steps on the way to reaching a desired goal when they are pursued with a clear aim in mind.

SMART Goals Framework:

Many experts advise adopting the SMART framework (Specific, Measurable, Achievable, Relevant, and Time-bound) to make sure financial objectives are effective. Clarity is eliminated by specificity, achievability guarantees realistic targets, measurability establishes a clear standard for achievement, relevance links objectives to personal values, and time-bound establishes an end date for completion. By using a systematic method, aspirations become more actionable and goal-setting becomes more effective.

Emergency Fund as a Foundation:

The creation of an emergency fund is one of the fundamental financial objectives that is frequently stressed. This fund serves as a safety net, offering financial stability in case of unforeseen events like job loss or urgent medical needs. It's generally advised that people put three to six months' worth of living expenses in a readily accessible account. This way, they may ensure that they can weather unforeseen storms without having to abandon their long-term financial plans.

Prioritizing Debt Repayment:

Debt can be a major barrier to financial well-being for a lot of people. As such, paying off debt is frequently at the core of important financial objectives. Credit card bills and other high-interest debts should be prioritised to reduce financial stress and free up funds for other objectives. A solid financial foundation is also made possible by the gratification of paying off debt.

Homeownership Dreams:

A popular long-term financial ambition and a fundamental component of the American Dream is property ownership. Achieving this objective will require putting money aside for a down payment and understanding the nuances of different mortgage alternatives. Aside from the financial benefits, becoming a homeowner frequently denotes security, stability, and a feeling of achievement.

Educational Pursuits:

Investing in one's own or one's family's education is another common financial objective. Putting money aside for books, tuition, and other related costs needs careful preparation. Education objectives can include accumulating money for a child's education fund or going back to school to improve one's employment opportunities. Pursuing education with a feeling of purpose is encouraged when these objectives are in line with a long-term vision.

Retirement Planning:

Retirement planning is one of the most important long-term financial objectives. The process of putting money aside for a safe and enjoyable retirement requires careful planning, investment management, and savings. Contributions to retirement accounts, such as 401(k)s and IRAs, have a compounding effect, so the earlier people start, the more time their investments have to grow.

Balancing Multiple Goals:

Many people find themselves balancing several financial objectives at once. Resolving conflicts between immediate and long-term goals necessitates carefully setting priorities. While taking care of present necessities is crucial, setting aside money for long-term objectives guarantees a secure and satisfying financial future. Dynamically reevaluating and modifying goals in response to changing circumstances is an essential component of sound financial planning.

Overcoming Challenges:

Reaching financial objectives is not always an easy journey. Challenges could come from unforeseen costs, changes in the market, and life occurrences. Nonetheless, the ability to bounce back from setbacks is a necessary quality for achieving goals. Overcoming obstacles on the path to achieving financial goals requires flexibility in responding to shifting conditions while adhering to the larger vision.

Celebrating Milestones:

Setting financial goals is about enjoying the road as much as the final destination. Celebrating accomplishments strengthens the good habits developed when pursuing financial objectives, whether they involve paying off a sizable debt, hitting a savings goal, or attaining a professional milestone. These festivities inspire further advancement.

Chapter One: Understanding Investment Basics

Types of investments

Choosing investments is like picking the foundation of a financial future. Individuals can increase their wealth, make money, and reach their financial objectives by investing in stocks, bonds, real estate, and a variety of other financial products.

1. Stocks: The Ownership Power:

Stocks are the foundation of many investing portfolios since they signify ownership in a company. A person who purchases stock in a firm shares in its achievements and failures, becoming a part owner of the business. The performance of the company, the state of the market, and economic variables can all affect the value of stocks.

Types of Stocks:

- **Common Stocks:** These are a common type of stock ownership that entitles

holders to dividends from the company's profits as well as voting rights.
· **Preferred Stocks:** Although preferred stock owners usually do not have voting rights, they do enjoy preference when it comes to dividends and liquidation.

Potential Rewards and Risks:

· **Potential Rewards:** Investing in stocks can yield significant profits, particularly in the long run. Additionally, businesses may pay dividends to their stockholders.
· **Risks:** Market speculation, prevailing economic conditions, and company-specific factors can all have an impact on how volatile stock values can be. The capital that has been invested could be lost.

2. Bonds: The Foundation of Fixed Income:

Bonds are financial securities in which investors essentially lend money to corporations, governments, or municipalities in return for regular interest payments and the principal amount returned when the bond matures. Because they offer a constant income stream, bonds are frequently regarded as being more conservative than stocks.

Types of Bonds:

· **Government Bonds:** Issued by governments to fund public projects, these are generally considered low-risk.
· **Corporate Bonds:** Issued by corporations to raise capital, offering higher yields but with increased risk.
· **Municipal Bonds:** Issued by state and local governments for public projects, providing tax advantages for investors.

Potential Rewards and Risks:

- *Potential Rewards:* Bonds provide a predictable income stream through interest payments and return of principal at maturity.
- *Risks:* Bond prices can be affected by changes in interest rates, credit risk, and inflation. In some cases, there's a risk of default, especially with lower-rated corporate bonds.

3. Real Estate: Building Wealth through Tangible Assets:

Investing in real estate involves purchasing properties with the aim of generating rental income or realizing capital appreciation. Real estate can provide both diversification and a hedge against inflation.

Types of Real Estate Investments:

- *Residential Real Estate:* Investing in single-family homes, condominiums, or multi-family properties for rental income.
- *Commercial Real Estate:* Involves properties like office buildings, retail spaces, and industrial facilities.
- *Real Estate Investment Trusts (REITs):* These are investment vehicles that allow individuals to invest in a diversified portfolio of real estate assets.

Potential Rewards and Risks:

- *Potential Rewards:* Real estate can offer a steady income stream through rental payments and the potential for property appreciation.
- *Risks:* Real estate investments require significant capital and can be illiquid. Market fluctuations, economic downturns, and property management challenges are risks to consider.

4. Mutual Funds: Diversification Made Accessible:

Mutual funds pool money from multiple investors to invest in a diversified portfolio of stocks, bonds, or other securities. They are managed by professional fund managers, providing investors with instant diversification.

Types of Mutual Funds:

- *Equity Funds:* Invest primarily in stocks, aiming for capital appreciation.
- *Fixed-Income Funds:* Focus on bonds and other fixed-income securities, providing income.
- *Index Funds:* Mimic the performance of a specific market index, offering broad market exposure.

Potential Rewards and Risks:

- *Potential Rewards:* Mutual funds offer diversification, professional management, and ease of access for individual investors.
- *Risks:* Fees and expenses can impact returns, and the performance of actively managed funds depends on the skill of the fund manager.

5. Exchange-Traded Funds (ETFs): Combining Flexibility and Diversification:

ETFs are similar to mutual funds but trade on stock exchanges like individual stocks. They offer diversification and flexibility, allowing investors to buy and sell throughout the trading day at market prices.

Types of ETFs:

- **Equity ETFs:** Track specific stock indices or sectors.
- **Bond ETFs:** Mirror the performance of bond indices or focus on specific fixed-income securities.

- **Commodity ETFs:** Invest in commodities like gold, oil, or agricultural products.

Potential Rewards and Risks:

- **Potential Rewards:** ETFs provide diversification, low expense ratios, and intraday trading flexibility.
- **Risks:** Like mutual funds, fees can impact returns. Additionally, the value of ETFs can fluctuate based on market conditions.

6. Cryptocurrencies: Navigating the Digital Frontier:

In recent years, cryptocurrencies have emerged as a new and innovative investment class. Bitcoin, Ethereum, and other digital currencies operate on blockchain technology and have gained attention for their potential as a store of value and medium of exchange.

Types of Cryptocurrencies:

- *Bitcoin (BTC):* Often referred to as digital gold, Bitcoin is the first and most well-known cryptocurrency.
- *Ethereum (ETH):* Known for its smart contract capabilities, Ethereum has a broader range of applications beyond being a digital currency.
- *Altcoins:* Refers to all other cryptocurrencies besides Bitcoin, including Ripple (XRP), Litecoin (LTC), and more.

Potential Rewards and Risks:

- **Potential Rewards:** Cryptocurrencies have shown potential for high returns, and blockchain technology has applications beyond digital currencies.
- **Risks:** Extreme price volatility, regulatory uncertainty, and the evolving nature of the cryptocurrency space pose risks. Security concerns and

market sentiment can also impact prices.

7. Precious Metals: Safeguarding Wealth in Tangible Form:

Investing in precious metals like gold and silver has been a traditional method of preserving wealth. These metals are considered a hedge against inflation and economic uncertainties.

Types of Precious Metal Investments:

- **Gold:** Often seen as a store of value, gold is used for both investment and industrial purposes.
- **Silver:** Has industrial uses and is also considered a precious metal investment.
- **Platinum and Palladium:** Used in industrial applications and as investment options.

Potential Rewards and Risks:

- **Potential Rewards:** Precious metals can act as a hedge against inflation and economic downturns. They are tangible assets with intrinsic value.
- **Risks:** Prices can be influenced by factors such as market speculation, geopolitical events, and industrial demand. Precious metals do not generate income like dividends or interest.

8. Savings Accounts and Certificates of Deposit (CDs): Stability and Safety:

While not traditionally viewed as investments, savings accounts and CDs offer stability and safety for individuals looking to preserve capital while earning interest.

Types of Savings and CD Options:

- **Savings Accounts:** Offer liquidity, allowing individuals to withdraw funds easily. Interest rates may vary.
- **Certificates of Deposit (CDs):** Typically offer higher interest rates but require funds to be locked in for a specific term.

Potential Rewards and Risks:

- **Potential Rewards:** Savings accounts and CDs provide safety of principal and are FDIC-insured (up to certain limits). CDs offer higher interest rates for longer-term commitments.
- **Risks:** Returns are generally lower compared to riskier investments like stocks. The impact of inflation on purchasing power is a consideration.

Risk and return

Risk and return have a relationship that is similar to a delicate dance, in which every move has an impact on the previous one. Knowing this dynamic interaction is essential for investors to build a strategy that fits their risk tolerance and personal objectives, not just from a financial standpoint.

Fundamentals: Definition of Risk and Return:

Fundamentally, risk is the unpredictability or possibility of loss connected to an investment. Conversely, return refers to the monetary profit or loss that an investment realizes over a given time frame. These two components are essential to investment decision-making since they are inseparably related.

The Risk-Return Spectrum:

In terms of risk and return, not all investments are made equal. The range of options open to investors, from low-risk, low-return options to high-risk, high-return possibilities, is depicted by the risk-return spectrum.

Low-Risk, Low-Return:

- **Cash and Equivalents:** While offering stability and liquidity, these typically provide minimal returns.
- **Government Bonds:** Considered low-risk, these provide relatively modest returns compared to riskier assets.

Medium-Risk, Medium-Return:

- **Diversified Portfolios:** Balanced asset allocations that include a mix of stocks and bonds fall into this category.
- **Real Estate Investment Trusts (REITs):** Combining elements of stocks and real estate, REITs offer moderate risk and potential returns.

High-Risk, High-Return:

- **Individual Stocks:** These can offer significant returns, but the volatility and uncertainty make them high-risk.
- **Cryptocurrencies:** Known for their potential for substantial gains, cryptocurrencies also come with high volatility and speculative risk.

The Balancing Act:

The constant challenge for any investor is to find a risk-return mix that fits both their comfort level and their financial objectives. Numerous elements influence this delicate balancing act:

1. **Risk Tolerance:** This is an individual's ability to endure fluctuations in the value of their investments. It's crucial to understand personal risk tolerance, as it varies from person to person.

2. **Investment Horizon:** The timeframe over which an individual plans to hold an investment plays a significant role. Longer investment horizons may allow for a higher tolerance for short-term volatility.

3. **Financial Objectives:** Various objectives call for various strategies. For retirement savings, a longer-term, growth-oriented strategy may be needed, whilst more conservative methods may be needed for short-term objectives.

Types of Risk:

Recognizing the different shapes that risk can take is essential to understanding it.

1. **Market Risk:** The risk of losses due to factors affecting the entire market, such as economic downturns or geopolitical events.

2. **Credit Risk:** The risk that an issuer of a bond or a borrower will fail to make timely interest payments or repay the principal amount

3. **Inflation Risk:** The risk that inflation will erode the purchasing power of money over time, impacting the real return on investments.

4. **Liquidity Risk:** The risk of not being able to quickly buy or sell an investment

at a fair price, potentially resulting in losses.

5. *Operational Risk:* The risk of losses due to internal failures, errors, or disruptions within an organization or financial institution.

The Search for Refunds:

Investors are generally faced with the fundamental notion that greater potential returns are usually accompanied by higher degrees of risk in their pursuit of returns. The core of the risk-return trade-off is this. While riskier assets may have the potential for higher returns, assets or investments that are thought to be safer typically generate lower returns.

1. *Diversification as a Risk Mitigation Strategy:*
   Diversification is the process of distributing investments among several industries, asset classes, and geographical areas. By lessening the impact of a single investment's bad performance, this can help decrease risk.

2. *Risk Tolerance and Emotional Resilience:* A thorough understanding of an investor's risk tolerance extends beyond simple numerical measures. During market downturns, a risk-averse person may become frightened, and rash decisions that could negatively impact long-term objectives may be made.

3. *The Impact of Time Horizon:* An investor's expectations for risk and return are greatly influenced by their time horizon. A longer time horizon permits the potential recovery from market downturns and the compounding of profits over time, even though short-term swings may be unpleasant.

Mitigating Risk:

Investing carries risk, but there are wise ways to lessen its effects:

1. *Research and Due Diligence:* Investors can make well-informed selections by doing extensive study on investments, comprehending market conditions, and maintaining up-to-date knowledge.

2. *Asset Allocation:* Dividing assets among several classes bonds, equities, and real estate, for example, helps minimize risk and maximize profits.

3. *Risk Management Techniques:* Using risk management techniques, such as stop-loss orders and hedging plans, can shield investments against losses in the market.

4. *Regular Portfolio Review:* By reviewing the investment portfolio regularly, you can make sure that it stays in line with your risk tolerance and financial objectives. Changes in circumstances may call for adjustments.

Diversification

Diversification is more than just a technique when it comes to investing; it's the conductor guiding a symphony of growth and stability in the financial world. A well-designed investment portfolio thrives on a variety of assets, much as a diversified garden does with a variety of plants.

The Significance of Diversification: A Comprehensive Method for Investing

Fundamentally, diversification refers to the process of distributing assets among different industries, geographical areas, asset classes, and financial instruments to establish a well-balanced portfolio. The objective is straightforward but effective: by avoiding excessive dependence on any one investment, the risk may be minimised and the return potential can be increased.

Consider a well-diversified portfolio as an intricately woven tapestry, where each thread represents a distinct investment or asset class. The interaction of these several components forges a strong fabric that withstands economic and market turbulence.

Diversification Beyond the Jargon: A Real-World Analogy

Think of diversification as a well-kept garden to help make it easier to understand. A wide variety of plants coexist in a garden; each has unique traits, advantages, and disadvantages. Consider growing just one kind of flower: a lovely, delicate bloom. The entire garden is vulnerable to bad weather or pest infestation. Now picture a garden with a variety of trees, shrubs, and flowers. Diversity adds durability in addition to improving the aesthetic appeal. When one species struggles, others flourish and the garden's general vitality is preserved.

Similar to this, a diverse portfolio in the context of investing consists of a variety of asset classes, such as stocks, bonds, real estate, and maybe alternative assets. Every element has a role in maintaining the overall stability and health of the portfolio, making it resilient to the inevitable ups and downs of the financial markets.

The Benefits of Diversification:

1. Risk Mitigation: One effective method of managing risks is diversification. The impact of a bad investment is lessened by the strong performance of other investments when money is dispersed over a variety of assets. It is a mechanism for risk mitigation that shields investors from the unwarranted impact of market volatility.

2. Stability in Volatile Markets: Economic cycles, geopolitical developments, and unforeseen events can all have an impact on financial markets' ups and downs. The purpose of a diverse portfolio is to offer stability in erratic times. Even while certain assets can lose value, others might hold up well or even grow in value, resulting in a performance that is balanced overall.

3. *Increased Potential for Returns:* Diversification tries to increase the potential for returns in addition to reducing risk. The performance patterns of various asset classes differ. Bonds give safety and income, whilst stocks can have room for growth. These components work together to maximize profits according to the investor's financial objectives and risk tolerance.

4. *Emotional Resilience:* Investing is not always a rational decision; feelings are frequently involved. Increasing diversity is essential for enhancing emotional resilience. A well-diversified portfolio can provide investors confidence during volatile market situations and assist them avoid making snap decisions out of fear or panic.

5. *Length-Term Wealth Accumulation:* Diversification is an effective strategy for wealth accumulation for investors with a lengthy time horizon. Investors can position themselves to profit from the potential of each component and contribute to long-term financial success by patiently allowing varied assets to grow and compound over time.

The Diversification Instruments:

A variety of investment vehicles are included in diversification, and each one contributes special features to the financial orchestra. The following essential elements are frequently included in a diversified portfolio:

1. *Stocks:* Known for their development potential, stocks symbolize ownership in businesses. Despite their potential for volatility, they play a significant role in the diversified portfolio and aid in capital growth.

2. Bonds: Bonds are debt instruments that provide interest payments as a steady source of revenue. They balance out the sometimes erratic nature of equities by offering steadiness.

3. *Real Estate:* Investing in real estate, whether in individual properties or Real

Estate Investment Trusts (REITs), gives the portfolio a tangible component. In addition to providing advantages for diversification, real estate can produce revenue through rental yields.

4. *Cash and Equivalents:* Money market funds and other cash equivalents give the portfolio stability and liquidity. They stabilize the market during downturns even if they could yield lesser rewards.

5. *Alternative Investments:* The Special Participants

Commodities, hedge funds, and private equity are examples of alternative investments that add some individuality to the diverse portfolio. These assets might perform differently from more conventional investments, which would add another level of diversification.

The Dance of Correlation: Understanding Relationships Between Assets

Knowing how different assets are correlated is essential to diversification's efficacy. The degree to which the prices of two assets fluctuate in connection to one another is measured by correlation. In a diversified portfolio, assets with low or negative correlation are especially beneficial.

Think about bonds and stocks, for instance. These two asset types haven't historically shown much of a positive link. Bonds may not enjoy large gains when stocks perform well, but they also tend not to face sharp drops. This low correlation makes diversification more effective and results in a smoother overall performance.

The Symphony of Rebalancing: Fine-Tuning for Harmony

Diversification is a continuous process that needs to be adjusted rather than a one-time setup. The initial portfolio balance may be changed by market swings, which could result in an excess or underexposure to particular assets. Rebalancing entails changing the distribution of assets to preserve the intended risk-return profile.

Envision a musical group where harmony is maintained by periodic tuning of each instrument. A varied portfolio also has to be adjusted regularly. A bull market may cause some assets to outperform, which would skew the allocation. To keep the portfolio in line with the investor's objectives, rebalancing entails selling some of the outperforming assets and reallocating funds to others who may have underperformed.

The Emotional Intelligence of Diversification:

For many people, investing is an emotional adventure as well as a mathematical game. To improve emotional intelligence when making financial decisions, diversification is essential. A diverse portfolio provides stability and lessens the chance of impulsive decisions stemming from feelings triggered by market fluctuations.

Imagine a situation when there is a sharp decline in the stock market. Although the value of an investor's stocks may drop in a well-diversified portfolio, the impact is lessened by the stability of other assets like bonds or real estate. This consistency might serve as a safeguard against rash actions that could jeopardize long-term financial objectives.

The Personalization of Diversification: Crafting Your Financial Symphony

Diversification is a customized process that matches each person's financial objectives, risk tolerance, and investment horizon rather than a one-size-fits-all approach. Each person has a different ideal combination of assets depending on their goals and particular situation.

Think about two investors whose levels of risk tolerance differ. A more substantial allocation to stocks may be made by Investor A, who has a larger risk tolerance and is looking for better growth potential. Investor B, on the other hand, might prioritize stability by maintaining a more balanced mix of equities and bonds due to their lower risk tolerance. Creating a portfolio that speaks to an investor's financial goals and offers a route to their particular idea of financial success is the art of diversification.

Challenges and Critiques: Navigating the Complexities of Diversification

Diversification is a great tactic, but it is not without problems and detractors. The risk of over-diversification, in which a portfolio has too many components and becomes unduly complex, is one prevalent criticism. Excessive diversity has the potential to lessen the return on profitable investments and complicate portfolio management.

The constantly changing nature of correlations presents another difficulty. Changes in market dynamics, economic conditions, or world events might cause asset classes that were previously thought to be minimally correlated to see changes in their correlations. It will take constant observation and modification to adjust to these changes.

Furthermore, diversity does not shield against losses or ensure returns, particularly in volatile markets. It is a risk management tactic that aims to raise the likelihood of long-term success without completely removing the inherent risks associated with investment.

Implementing Diversification: A Step-by-Step Guide

Applying diversity calls for a methodical and deliberate strategy. This is a comprehensive how-to guide for creating a diversified portfolio:

1. *Set Financial Goals:* Establish your financial objectives first. Are you putting money down for your kids' school, your own house, or retirement? Your investing horizon and risk tolerance will be influenced by your objectives.

2. *Assess Risk Tolerance:* Recognise how much you can withstand changes in the value of your investments. A financial advisor's advice or the use of a risk assessment tool can provide you with information about your risk tolerance.

3. *Determine Investment Horizon:* Take into account your investment horizon, or the period you intend to hold onto your investments. A more growth-oriented approach might be possible with longer time horizons.

4. *Select Diverse Asset Classes:* Assign your goals, risk tolerance, and investment horizon to a variety of asset classes. Alternative investments, real estate, bonds, and stocks are examples of common asset classes.

5. *Understand Correlation:* Examine past correlations between selected asset types. Choose a mix of assets that move independently of one another and provide good diversification.

6. *Allocate Funds:* Using your preferred risk-return ratio, distribute your assets among the chosen asset groups. Selecting the portion of your portfolio allocated to each asset type is the task for this stage.

7. *Regularly Rebalance:* Examine your portfolio regularly and adjust it as necessary. The initial allocation may change due to market volatility; rebalancing makes sure your portfolio stays within your targeted risk-return range.

8. *Stay Informed:* Remain up to date on world events, market conditions, and economic trends. Maintaining your expertise gives you the ability to make wise judgments regarding your portfolio.

9. *Seek Professional Advice:* Take into Account Speaking with a Financial Advisor. Their knowledge can offer insightful advice on how to create a diversified portfolio that is specific to your financial situation.

Case Study: Implementing Diversification

Now, let's investigate a fictitious case study to demonstrate the value of diversification. Consider Sarah, an investor, who first puts all of her money into technology stocks. Gradually, the technology industry undergoes a recession, leading to substantial losses for Sarah's investment portfolio.

Imagine now a different scenario where bonds and real estate investment trusts (REITs) are added to Sarah's portfolio in addition to technology stocks. The stability and income from bonds and real estate helped to offset Sarah's portfolio losses during the collapse in the technology sector. Sarah gains from the potential upside when the technology sector rebounds and her diversified portfolio weathers the storm more skillfully.

The benefits of diversification in terms of resilience and risk mitigation are emphasized in this case study. The diversified approach guarantees that the entire portfolio remains robust even in the face of challenges faced by individual industries or assets.

Chapter Two : Financial Planning

Creating a budget

C reating a budget is akin to composing a symphony for your financial well-being. It's not just about numbers on a spreadsheet; it's a dynamic process that empowers you to orchestrate your income, expenses, and savings in harmony with your life goals.

The Core of Financial Well-Being: Comprehending the Significance of Budgeting

Fundamentally, a budget serves as a road map for your financial journey, offering an organized strategy for the distribution of your assets. It's a tool that assists you in prudent money management, helping you to reach your long-term financial objectives while making sure you have enough for necessities and wants.

Consider your budget as the maestro of an orchestra, expertly guiding every financial instrument's income, expenses, and savings to produce a melodious tune. Understanding and embracing the fundamentals of budgeting gives you the ability to take charge of your financial story and make deliberate decisions that align with your goals.

The Human Aspect of Financial Planning

Although budgeting is mostly a human endeavor, it does require statistics and calculations. It is an expression of your priorities, values, and desired way of life. Your budgeting method gains personalization when you include the human aspect; this makes the approach more sustainable and tailored to your particular situation.

Think of your budget as an empowerment tool rather than a constraint. It enables you to allocate your resources thoughtfully, promoting financial independence and lowering stress levels. When you take into account the human factor, budgeting becomes less of a chore and more of a constructive and empowering activity.

The Components of a Comprehensive Budget: Crafting Your Financial Symphony

A thorough budget consists of multiple essential elements, each of which is vital to the overall structure of your finances. Let's examine each of these parts in more detail:

1. Income:

- Start by recording all of your revenue sources, such as your pay, bonuses, earnings from freelancing, and any additional sources of funding.
- To portray your financial resources realistically, take into account both regular and irregular revenue sources.

2. Fixed Expenses:

- Determine your fixed expenses, which include necessary expenditures like utilities, insurance, rent or mortgage payments, and loan repayments.
- These are regular, ongoing costs that serve as the cornerstone of your spending plan.

3. *Variable Expenses:*

- Discretionary spending on non-essential things like eating out, enter-tainment, and shopping is included in the category of variable expenses.
- Even if these costs are flexible, careful *management* of them helps you reach your financial objectives.

4. *Savings:*

- Set aside a portion of your salary for savings, such as retirement accounts, emergency money, and targeted savings objectives.
- The future-focused part of your budget is represented by your savings, which guarantee the stability and security of your finances.

5. *Debt Repayment:*

- If you have any unpaid debts, like loans or credit card bills, set aside money in your budget for debt repayment.
- Making debt repayment a priority improves your financial situation and hastens the process of achieving financial freedom.

6. *Financial Goals:*

- Whether your financial objectives are to travel the world, purchase a property, or finance college, make a list and prioritize them.
- Set aside money in your budget for these objectives, and they will go from being dreams to real accomplishments.

The Art of Budgeting: Crafting a Vision for Your Financial Future

1. *Reflect on Your Values:*

- Give careful thought to your ideals and financial goals before analyzing the numbers. What is most important to you? What are your long- and short-term objectives?

- Your budget will become a tool for leading a happy and purposeful life if it is in line with your ideals.

2. Set Realistic Goals:

- Set attainable and reasonable financial objectives. Having specific goals gives your budget direction, whether it's for debt repayment, vacation savings, or emergency fund building.
- Since realistic goals are more likely to be maintained over time, they improve your financial health overall.

3. Track Your Spending:

- Begin by keeping a tab on your expenses for a predetermined amount of time, such as a few weeks or a month. This procedure offers insightful information about your spending habits.
- Spreadsheets and budgeting software are useful tools for classifying spending and pinpointing areas that need tweaking.

4. Categorize Your Expenses:

- Separate your costs into categories based on what is fixed and what is variable. This classification facilitates the process of creating a budget by making it easier to spot possible areas for savings.
- Housing, utilities, groceries, transit, entertainment, and other sporadic costs are typical categories.

5. Prioritize Debt Repayment:

- Make debt repayment a top priority if you have any outstanding bills. Think about the avalanche or snowball approach, paying off one debt at a

time.
- In addition to strengthening your financial position, paying off debt frees up funds for other objectives.

6. Emergency Fund:

- Set aside some money in your budget to create and keep an emergency fund. This fund acts as a safety net for finances in the event of unforeseen costs or interruptions.
- To improve your financial resilience, aim to have three to six months' worth of living expenditures in your emergency fund.

Addressing Common Budgeting Challenges: Navigating the Complexity of Your Financial Composition

Although creating a budget is not always easy, overcoming these typical obstacles is crucial to creating a long-term financial plan:

1. Unexpected Expenses:

- Acknowledge that unforeseen costs are unavoidable. Add wiggle room to your budget so that unanticipated events won't negatively affect your total spending plan.

2. Irregular Income:

- Make a budget based on a cautious estimate of your average monthly income if your income is erratic. Make use of the fluctuations to save savings for when earnings are very strong.

3. Lifestyle Adjustments:

- Accept that as your financial status changes, you may need to make lifestyle adjustments. Be willing to review and change your budget as needed to accommodate evolving needs and objectives.

4. Budgeting Burnout:

- Burnout is a regular issue and budgeting calls for constant work. To avoid burnout, incorporate aspects of self-compassion and flexibility into your budgeting process.
- To keep a healthy balance, acknowledge little accomplishments and permit yourself to occasionally indulge.

5. Overcoming Debt:

- Paying off debts can take time to complete. Divide your debt payback objectives into doable benchmarks and acknowledge each small victory as you go.
- If necessary, look for assistance from debt management programmes or financial counselors.

The Ongoing Symphony: Regular Review and Adjustment

A budget is a dynamic tool that needs to be reviewed and adjusted regularly; it is not a static document. The success of your budget can be impacted by external influences, financial objectives, and life situations. Continually reviewing and adjusting your budget guarantees that it is in line with your changing financial situation.

1. Monthly Check-Ins:

- Plan on reviewing the performance of your budget every month. Examine your actual spending and your planned spending to find any differences or potential areas for improvement.
- Make use of periodic check-ins to recognize accomplishments, review

objectives, and make any adjustments.

2. Life Changes and Adjustments:

- Because life is dynamic, changes in circumstances should be reflected in your budget. Whether your priorities are changing financially, moving careers, or adding a family, make the necessary adjustments to your budget.
- Maintaining the relevance and efficacy of your budget in directing your financial decisions is ensured by updating it in response to life events.

3. Emergency Fund Maintenance:

- Examine and reload your emergency savings regularly. Your emergency fund should be increased or decreased in proportion to your current living expenses as your financial condition changes.
- Having a sufficiently large emergency fund strengthens your ability to withstand financial shocks when they arise.

Budgeting Tools and Resources: Enhancing Your Symphony with Technology

Utilise technology to improve the way you create budgets. There are a plethora of tools and resources at your disposal to streamline the procedure and offer insightful information about your financial orchestration:

1. Budgeting Apps:

- Explore budgeting apps like Mint, YNAB (You Need A Budget), or Pocket-Guard. These apps link to your accounts, categorize expenses, and provide real-time insights into your financial situation.
- Mobile apps make budgeting accessible and convenient, allowing you to track expenses on the go.

2. *Spreadsheets:*

- For those who prefer a more hands-on approach, traditional budgeting spreadsheets, such as those in Microsoft Excel or Google Sheets, offer customization and flexibility.
- Create your budgeting template or explore pre-designed templates available online.

3. Financial Advisors:

- Consider seeking guidance from a financial advisor. A professional can provide personalized insights, help set realistic financial goals, and assist in crafting a budget tailored to your unique circumstances.
- Financial advisors offer expertise in optimizing your budget for long-term financial success.

4. Online Resources:

- Explore online resources and educational materials dedicated to budgeting and personal finance. Websites like Investopedia, NerdWallet, and The Balance offer guides, articles, and tools to deepen your financial knowledge.
- Engaging with online communities and forums can provide support and insights from individuals facing similar financial challenges.

Budgeting for Different Life Stages: Adapting Your Symphony to Life's Progression

Your budget changes as you move through different periods of life; it is not a one-size-fits-all structure. Take into account the particular financial factors at each step and modify your budget as necessary:

1. **Early Career:** In the early stages of your career, focus on building a strong financial foundation. Allocate funds towards emergency savings, debt repayment, and investment in skills and education.

2. **Family Planning:** As you plan for or expand your family, adjust your budget to accommodate shared financial responsibilities. Include categories for childcare, education savings, and family-related expenses.

3. **Mid-Career:** During the mid-career phase, leverage your earning potential to bolster savings and investments. Reassess your budget to align with advancing career goals, homeownership aspirations, and retirement planning.

4. **Empty Nest:** As children leave the nest, reallocate resources to focus on retirement savings, travel, and personal interests. This stage often provides more financial flexibility to pursue long-held passions.

5. **Retirement:** In retirement, your budget shifts to prioritize sustaining your desired lifestyle. Emphasize ongoing savings, healthcare costs, and potential travel or leisure activities.

The Emotional Dimension of Budgeting: Nurturing a Positive Financial Mindset

Budgeting takes into account the emotional aspect of financial wellness in addition to the numbers. Building a sound financial mindset is essential to creating a good budget:

1. Shift from Restriction to Empowerment:

- Reframe your perspective on budgeting from a restrictive practice to an empowering tool. Recognize that a budget provides the freedom to allocate resources in alignment with your goals.

2. Celebrate Small Wins:

- Celebrate small victories along your budgeting journey. Whether it's consistently sticking to your budget for a month or achieving a savings goal, acknowledge and celebrate these milestones

3. Practice Self-Compassion:

- Budgeting is a learning process, and mistakes may occur. Practice self-compassion and view setbacks as opportunities for growth. Adjust your budget as needed and continue refining your financial practices.

4. Engage in Open Communication:

- If budgeting involves shared financial responsibilities, maintain open communication with family members or partners. Collaborative budgeting fosters a sense of shared goals and accountability.

Emergency funds

The emergency fund is one of the most important and well-balanced compositions in the grand orchestration of personal finance. A safeguard, a buffer, and a lifeline during unforeseen turns and turns is provided by this financial safety net.

The Essence of an Emergency Fund

An emergency fund is more than just a stash of cash; it serves as a buffer against unforeseen obstacles in life and offers stability and security during difficult times. Fundamentally, an emergency fund is a collection of liquid assets, such as easily available cash or its equivalents, placed aside especially to handle unforeseen costs or financial difficulties.

Consider your emergency fund as a guardian angel, ready to shield you from unforeseen financial storms that life may bring. Having a well-funded emergency fund guarantees you can weather these hardships without jeopardizing your overall financial stability, whether it's an unexpected medical bill, auto repairs, or job loss.

The Importance of an Emergency Fund

1. Protection Against the Unexpected: Because life is unpredictable by nature, unforeseen costs are a fact of life. As a kind of financial safety net, an emergency fund provides security against unanticipated events like medical crises, home maintenance, or vehicle problems.

2. Stability During Income Disruptions: An emergency fund offers stability and peace of mind during uncertain times such as job loss or interruption of income. It acts as a safety net, paying for necessities while you work through the difficulties of finding new employment or establishing a steady income.

3.Prevention of Debt Accumulation: Without an emergency fund, individuals might borrow money or take on debt to cover unforeseen expenses. A vicious cycle of debt and financial strain may result from this. Having a sufficient emergency reserve keeps you from having to rely on high-interest loans or credit cards.

4. _Enhanced Decision-Making:_ Having a safety net helps you make wiser choices when things get hard financially. Instead of being constrained by sudden financial difficulties, you may concentrate on identifying possibilities and solutions.

5. _Reduced Stress and Anxiety:_ For many individuals, financial stress is a major cause of anxiety. Establishing an emergency fund relieves this pressure, enabling you to face life's bumps with more poise and fortitude.

6. _Fostering Long-Term Financial Health:_ An emergency fund is a crucial component of long-term financial stability, not merely a temporary fix. You may build a strong foundation for pursuing other financial objectives, like investing, saving for retirement, or becoming a homeowner, by having a safety net.

The Human Element of Emergency Funds: Nurturing Financial Wellness with Compass

Although the value of an emergency fund is obvious, its function in promoting overall financial well-being is enhanced by the human element, which gives it depth and compassion:

Self-compassion: Creating and keeping an emergency fund is a self-compassionate gesture. It recognizes that difficulties will inevitably come and that life is unpredictable. You show that you care about your future self by taking proactive steps to prepare for these obstacles.

Empowerment through Advance Planning: Possessing an emergency fund gives you the ability to prepare for and overcome financial difficulties. The experience of unforeseen expenses is turned from a catastrophe into a scenario that can be managed with this sense of empowerment.

Mindful Financial Decision-Making: Having an emergency fund on hand promotes careful decision-making. It makes you think about how different decisions may affect your finances, which encourages you to manage your resources with caution and responsibility.

Strength in Financial Independence: Financial independence is facilitated by having an emergency reserve. Having your resources when you need them helps you feel more independent and less dependent on other people for financial support.

Cultivating a Positive Financial Mindset: Creating and preserving an emergency fund is an investment in sound financial planning. It displays a proactive attitude to money management by placing more emphasis on readiness and fortitude than on financial tactics that are reactive.

Building Your Emergency Fund: The Art of Composition

1. Set a Realistic Goal: First, decide on a reasonable target for your emergency savings. Aiming for three to six months' worth of living expenses is a typical recommendation. You should modify this according to your situation, level of risk tolerance, and job security.

2. Start Small and Be Consistent: Start modestly if the thought of amassing a sizeable emergency fund seems daunting. The secret is to be consistent; set aside a certain amount from each paycheck for your emergency fund and build it up over time.

3. Automate Your Savings: By setting up automatic payments to your emergency fund, you can integrate savings into your everyday finances. Establish automatic transfers to an emergency savings account from your bank account.

4. *Prioritize High-Interest Debt Repayment:* If you have high-interest debt, you might want to prioritize paying it off in addition to setting up an emergency fund. Strike a balance that will let you accomplish both objectives while avoiding being unduly burdened by interest payments.

5. *Allocate Windfalls Wisely:* Windfalls are a great way to increase your emergency fund. Examples of these are tax returns and bonuses. Rather than overspending, use a part of your unexpected profits to strengthen your safety net.

6.*Review and Modify:* Reassess your emergency fund objective regularly and make any revisions. Changes in life circumstances, income, or spending patterns may make it necessary to review and adjust your goal.

Choosing the Right Shelter for Your Emergency Fund: Liquid Assets and Accessibility

An emergency fund's usefulness depends on how easily accessible it is in an emergency. Choosing liquid assets means you can be sure you have money saved up for unforeseen expenses. Think about the following choices:

1. *Savings Accounts:* Conventional savings accounts provide a safe and convenient choice for your emergency fund. Savings accounts are a popular option because of their reliability and liquidity, even though their return rates may not be as high as those of other assets.

2. *Money Market Accounts:* Aspects of checking and savings accounts are combined in money market accounts. They usually provide convenient access to cash and offer interest rates that are higher than those of traditional savings accounts.

3. *Certificates of Deposit (CDs):* CDs are time deposits with set interest rates and terms. They could have penalties for early withdrawal even though they have higher interest rates than savings accounts. Think about the trade-off between increased liquidity and interest rates.

4. *Short-Term Treasury Bonds:* Short-term Treasury bonds, in particular, offer a balance between yield and safety. They might not be as instantly accessible as typical savings accounts, even though they might have somewhat better interest rates.

5. *Avoiding High-Risk Investments:* Stability and accessibility are an emergency fund's main objectives. Steer clear of assets with volatile values or high risk of loss because they might not be dependable sources of money in an emergency.

Maintaining and Replenishing: The Ongoing Symphony of Financial Resilience

Creating an emergency fund is a continuous process that needs constant care and attention to be successful:

1. *Frequent Evaluations:* Make sure your emergency fund is still covering your living needs by regularly evaluating it. A new job or a move are two examples of life events that could affect your financial needs.

2.*Replenishment After Use:* Prioritize reloading your emergency fund if you must use it to cover unforeseen costs. Resuming consistent contributions can help you rebuild your financial safety net and keep it functional for future demands.

3. *Adjustments Based on Life Changes:* Since life is dynamic, things might change in your financial circumstances. Review your emergency fund target regularly in light of any changes to your family's needs, income, or expenses.

4. *Consideration of Economic Conditions:* If you want to add more protection against long-term financial difficulties, you might want to reevaluate your emergency fund objective during times of economic uncertainty, such as recessions or changes in the employment market.

Common Misconceptions and Clarifications: Navigating the Complexity of Emergency Fund Myths

1. *Myth: Emergency Funds Are Only for Job Loss:*

- Clarification: While job loss is a significant reason to tap into your emergency fund, it is not the only one. Unexpected medical expenses, car repairs, or home maintenance are also valid reasons. An emergency fund is versatile and covers various financial challenges.

2. *Myth: Only the Wealthy Need Emergency Funds:*

- Clarification: Emergency funds are essential for individuals across all income levels. Financial setbacks can happen to anyone, and having a safety net is crucial for maintaining stability and avoiding unnecessary debt.

3. *Myth: Credit Cards Can Serve as Emergency Funds:*

- Clarification: Relying solely on credit cards for emergencies can lead to high-interest debt. While credit cards can provide temporary relief, they should not replace the role of an emergency fund in providing immediate, interest-free access to funds.

4. *Myth: Having Insurance Eliminates the Need for an Emergency Fund:*

- Clarification: While insurance provides valuable protection, it may not cover all expenses or offer immediate access to funds. An emergency fund complements insurance by providing flexibility and covering a broader range of unforeseen circumstances.

5. Myth: Emergency Funds Are Set-and-Forget:

- Clarification: Building an emergency fund requires ongoing attention. Life changes, economic conditions, and fluctuations in expenses may necessitate adjustments to your emergency fund goal or contribution amounts.

4

Chapter Three: Choosing the Right Investment Strategy

Long-term vs. short-term goals

I n the orchestration of our lives, goals act as the sheet music, guiding our journey and shaping the composition of our aspirations. Two prominent players in this symphony are long-term and short-term goals, each contributing a unique melody to the overarching composition.

Defining the Players: Long-Term and Short-Term Goals

Let's define these players before we get lost in the harmonious interplay of short- and long-term goals:

Long-Term Goals: Long-term goals are the distant constellations on life's horizon. They typically span years, if not decades, and represent significant achievements or milestones. Examples include buying a home, saving for retirement, or achieving career mastery.

Short-Term Goals: Short-term goals, on the other hand, are the notes on the sheet music that contribute to the immediate rhythm of life. These goals are achievable in the near future, often within days, weeks, or months. Short-term goals could involve saving for a vacation, completing a project at work, or learning a new skill.

Understanding the Roles of Long-Term and Short-Term Goals

Long-Term Goals:

- *Vision and Direction:* Long-term goals serve as guiding stars, providing a sense of direction in the vast expanse of life. They represent the overarching vision of what you aspire to achieve over the course of your lifetime.
- *Sustainability and Legacy:* These goals are foundational elements that contribute to the sustainability and legacy you wish to create. Whether it's building financial security, nurturing meaningful relationships, or leaving a lasting impact, long-term goals shape the narrative of your life

Short-Term Goals:

- *Achievable Milestones:* Short-term goals are the tangible milestones that contribute to the realization of long-term aspirations. They break down the larger vision into manageable, achievable steps, providing a sense of progress and accomplishment.
- *Motivation and Momentum:* Achieving short-term goals generates momentum and fuels motivation. These immediate wins contribute to a positive feedback loop, propelling you forward on your journey and reinforcing your commitment to the overarching vision.

Balancing Act: The Interplay Between Long-Term and Short-Term Goals

1. Setting the Stage: Defining Long-Term Goals

- **Reflection and Clarity:** Begin by reflecting on your values, passions, and overarching aspirations. Long-term goals require a deep understanding of what truly matters to you, providing the clarity needed to set meaningful and authentic objectives.
- **SMART Criteria:** Utilize the SMART criteria (Specific, Measurable, Achievable, Relevant, Time-Bound) to structure your long-term goals. This framework ensures that your aspirations are well-defined and grounded in reality

2. Building the Foundation: The Role of Short-Term Goals

- **Breakdown and Sequencing:** Short-term goals act as the building blocks of long-term success. Break down your long-term goals into smaller, actionable steps. These short-term objectives create a sequential path, making the larger vision more manageable and achievable.
- **Flexibility and Adaptability:** Short-term goals offer flexibility and adaptability. Life is dynamic, and circumstances may change. Short-term objectives allow you to adjust your course, responding to unexpected challenges or opportunities without compromising the overall vision.

3. Dynamic Interaction: The Dance of Adaptation

- **Regular Assessment:** Regularly assess your progress towards both long-term and short-term goals. This ongoing evaluation ensures that your actions align with your overarching vision and allows for adjustments based on evolving circumstances.
- **Celebrate Achievements:** Celebrate the achievement of short-term goals as they contribute to the larger tapestry of your long-term vision. Acknowl-

edge the milestones, no matter how small, and use them as motivational fuel for the journey ahead.

Long-Term Goals: Crafting the Masterpiece of a Lifetime

1. *Financial Security and Independence:*

- *Homeownership:* Having a home is frequently one of the long-term financial objectives. In addition to housing, owning a home gives one a feeling of security and an asset that will likely increase in value with time.
- *Retirement Planning:* The foundation of long-term financial planning is retirement savings. It guarantees financial security and the peace of mind to enjoy your later years.

2. *Career Success and Personal Development:*

- Professional Development: Ongoing education and professional growth are essential components of long-term career objectives. A satisfying career path can be achieved through learning new skills, obtaining advanced degrees, or moving up the corporate ladder. Career mastery is one factor in this.
- *Entrepreneurial Ventures:* Long-term objectives for someone with an entrepreneurial spirit can include launching and expanding a profitable company. This endeavor calls for commitment, tenacity, and a well-thought-out plan.

3. *Personal Fulfilment and Meaningful Relationships:*

- *Family and Relationships:* Establishing and fostering deep connections is frequently at the center of long-term life objectives. This covers family planning, developing close friendships, and making constructive contributions to your community.

- **Personal Fulfilment and Passion Pursuit:** Long-term goals encompass more than just material success; they also include personal fulfillment. A meaningful life prioritizes well-being, pursues passions, and participates in activities.

Short-Term Goals: The Flourishes in the Daily Symphony

1. Savings and Financial Discipline:

- **Emergency Fund:** Establishing an emergency fund is one of your short-term financial objectives. This short-term goal offers a safety net in terms of finances, making sure you are ready for unforeseen costs.
- **Debt Repayment:** A short-term financial objective that supports long-term financial stability is repaying high-interest debt. It releases funds for savings and future investments.

2. Career Advancement and Skill Enhancement:

- **Project Completion:** In the professional sphere, short-term objectives frequently entail finishing particular projects or tasks. These successes add to a group's or organization's overall success.
- **Skill Acquisition:** Acquiring new abilities is a short-term objective that expands your professional toolbox. Continuous skill improvement, whether via seminars, classes, or on-the-job training, is essential for career advancement.

3. Health and Well-Being:

- **Fitness and Nutrition:** These two areas may be crucial to your short-term health objectives. Having clear goals for increasing physical activity or making dietary changes enhances general well-being.
- **Stress Management:** Setting aside time for self-care and stress manage-

ment is a short-term goal that has a good effect on mental and emotional well-being. Daily well-being is aided by routine breaks and mindfulness exercises.

Common Challenges and Strategies for Success

1. *Challenge: Overemphasis on Either Long-Term or Short-Term Goals*

- **Strategy:** *Integration and Alignment:* Strike a balance by integrating short-term goals that align with your long-term vision. Avoid the trap of solely focusing on immediate gratification or solely fixating on distant aspirations. A harmonious approach ensures a well-rounded and sustainable journey.

2. *Challenge: Unrealistic Expectations and Burnout*

- **Strategy:** *Realistic Planning and Self-Care:* Set realistic expectations for both long-term and short-term goals. Recognize that the journey is a marathon, not a sprint. Prioritize self-care, ensuring you maintain the energy and resilience needed for sustained progress.

3. *Challenge: Lack of Adaptability to Change*

- **Strategy:** *Flexibility and Openness:* Embrace flexibility and openness to change. Life is dynamic, and unforeseen circumstances may necessitate adjustments to your goals. Be adaptable without losing sight of your overarching vision.

4. *Challenge: Inadequate Planning and Organization*

- **Strategy:** *Effective Planning and Time Management:* Invest time in effective planning and organization. Break down long-term goals into manageable short-term tasks, create realistic timelines, and employ effective time management strategies to ensure steady progress.

Conservative vs. aggressive strategies

In the vast ocean of financial decision-making, the choice between conservative and aggressive investment strategies serves as a compass, guiding individuals on their journey toward financial goals. Each strategy carries its own set of currents, risks, and potential rewards, shaping the financial landscape in distinct ways.

Defining the Strategies: Conservative and Aggressive Investments

1. *Conservative Investment Strategy:*

- *Capital Preservation:* The fundamental idea of conservative investment is the preservation of capital. The protection of the initial investment is given priority in this strategy, which emphasizes lower-risk investments that yield steady returns.
- *Low Volatility:* The chance of notable value swings is decreased in conservative portfolios because they typically exhibit lower volatility. This stability promises a more predictable financial journey by protecting investors from sharp market declines.
- *Income generating:* One of the main components of conservative strategies is the generating of income through interest and dividends. A consistent income stream can be achieved by investments in cash equivalents, bonds, and dependable dividend-paying equities.

2. *Aggressive Investment Strategy:*

- *Capital Appreciation:* Focusing on capital appreciation is closely related to aggressive investing. By accepting greater degrees of risk, this strategy aims to increase returns. It frequently involves investing in growth stocks, emerging markets, and other high-potential but erratic assets.

- **High Volatility:** Generally speaking, aggressive portfolios are more volatile, exposing investors to larger swings in the market. Even though there is a danger associated with this volatility, there are also chances for large gains, particularly in the long run.
- **Focus on Long-Term Growth:** Aggressive methods take a long-term view, hoping to take advantage of compounding to build significant wealth. These portfolios may tolerate transient fluctuations in the hopes of achieving higher total returns.

The Human Element: Motivations and Emotions

Conservative Approach:

- **Motivations:** Individuals opting for a conservative investment approach are often motivated by a desire for financial stability and reduced anxiety about market fluctuations. The emphasis is on preserving wealth and minimizing the emotional toll of financial uncertainty.
- **Emotional Nuances:** The emotional journey of conservative investors is characterized by a sense of security and peace of mind. While the returns may be moderate, the lower volatility provides a comfort zone, allowing investors to navigate their financial seas with a steady hand.

Aggressive Approach:

- **Motivations:** Aggressive investors are often driven by a hunger for higher returns and the excitement of chasing growth opportunities. The allure of potential wealth creation and the willingness to embrace risk characterize the motivations behind aggressive investment choices.
- **Emotional Nuances:** The emotional landscape of aggressive investing involves a blend of excitement, anticipation, and a higher tolerance for uncertainty. While the journey may be marked by occasional turbulence,

the potential for significant rewards fuels a sense of thrill and accomplishment.

Considerations in Strategy Selection: Aligning with Financial Goals

1. Conservative Strategy:

- **Preservation of Wealth:** Conservative strategies are well-suited for those with a primary goal of preserving wealth. Individuals nearing retirement or seeking a low-risk approach to their investments may find comfort in the stability offered by conservative portfolios.
- **Income Needs:** If a steady stream of income is a priority, conservative investments that generate dividends and interest may align with the financial goals of those relying on investment income for living expenses.

2. Aggressive Strategy:

- **Long-Term Goals:** Aggressive strategies align with long-term growth objectives. Investors with a substantial time horizon, such as younger individuals saving for retirement, may opt for an aggressive approach to harness the power of compounding over an extended period.
- **Risk Appetite:** A higher risk appetite is a key consideration for those leaning towards aggressive strategies. Individuals comfortable with market volatility and able to withstand short-term losses may be better suited for the potential higher returns associated with aggressive investing.

Risk and Reward: A Balancing Act

1. Conservative Strategy:

- **Lower Returns:** One of the trade-offs in conservative investing is the potential for lower returns compared to aggressive strategies. The emphasis on capital preservation often translates to more modest growth.

· **Reduced Volatility:** The trade-off, however, comes with reduced volatility and a smoother financial journey. Conservative investors accept the trade-off of lower returns for the comfort of knowing that their portfolios are less susceptible to market turbulence.

2. Aggressive Strategy:

· **Higher Returns:** Aggressive investors accept the challenge of higher volatility in exchange for the potential of higher returns. The pursuit of capital appreciation and significant wealth creation comes with the understanding that the journey may involve sharper market swings.

· **Embracing Risk:** Embracing risk is an inherent aspect of aggressive investing. While the potential for substantial rewards exists, so does the risk of significant losses. Aggressive investors must navigate this landscape with a well-defined risk management strategy.

Strategic Tools: Diversification and Asset Allocation

1. Conservative Strategy:

· **Diversification:** Diversification is a key tool in conservative investing. By spreading investments across different asset classes, conservative portfolios aim to reduce risk and enhance stability. Common components include bonds, stable dividend stocks, and cash equivalents.

· **Asset Allocation:** Conservative asset allocation often leans towards a higher percentage of fixed-income securities, providing a predictable income stream and a buffer against market volatility.

1. Aggressive Strategy:

· **Diversification with a Growth Focus:** Aggressive portfolios also leverage diversification but with a focus on growth-oriented assets. This may include a higher allocation to growth stocks, technology sectors, and emerging markets to capture opportunities for capital appreciation.

· **Strategic Asset Allocation:** The asset allocation in aggressive strategies is designed to align with the pursuit of long-term growth. Equities, especially those with high growth potential, may constitute a larger portion of the portfolio.

Market Conditions and Investor Psychology

1. Conservative Strategy:

· **Market Downturns:** Conservative investors may experience more stability during market downturns. The emphasis on capital preservation and lower-risk assets helps cushion the impact of economic uncertainties.

· **Psychological Comfort:** During challenging market conditions, conservative investors often experience psychological comfort, knowing that their portfolios are less susceptible to dramatic declines.

2. Aggressive Strategy:

· **Potential for Higher Losses:** Aggressive investors may face higher losses during market downturns due to the higher volatility of their portfolios. The potential for significant declines is a trade-off for the pursuit of higher long-term returns.

· **Resilience and Confidence:** The psychological landscape of aggressive investors involves a level of resilience and confidence in their ability to weather market fluctuations. The awareness of potential volatility is balanced by a belief in the strategy's potential for growth.

5

Chapter Four: Investment Vehicles

Stock market investments

I n the realm of personal finance, stock market investments stand as a captivating and often dynamic avenue for wealth creation. Beyond the numbers and market trends, the journey of investing in stocks is deeply intertwined with human emotions, aspirations, and the pursuit of financial goals.

The Human Element: Motivations and Emotional Landscape

1. Motivations Behind Stock Market Investments:

- **Wealth Accumulation:** The desire to accumulate money is the driving force behind stock market investments. To increase their financial resources for retirement, school, or other long-term goals, individuals frequently look to the stock market.
- **Financial Independence:** The pursuit of financial independence is a powerful motivator. Stock market investments offer the potential to generate passive income and achieve a level of financial autonomy, allowing individuals to make choices based on personal fulfillment rather

than financial constraints.

2. *Emotional Nuances of Stock Market Investing*:

- *Optimism and Excitement:* Investing in the stock market is frequently accompanied by optimism and excitement. It might be stimulating to consider the possibility of possible profits and the attraction of taking part in the expansion of reputable businesses.
- *Fear and Anxiety:* On the other hand, anxiety can be brought on by worry of market declines and the possibility of financial loss. The emotional rollercoaster of market swings can put investors' commitment to the test, particularly in tumultuous times.

Understanding the Stock Market: A Blend of Art and Science

1. *The Art of Timing: Navigating Market Trends*

- *Market Timing Challenges:* Timing the market is considered an art, and it poses challenges for even the most seasoned investors. The unpredictability of market movements makes it challenging to consistently buy or sell stocks at the most opportune moments.
- *Patience as a Virtue:* Successful investors often emphasize the virtue of patience. The art lies in resisting the urge to react impulsively to short-term market fluctuations and maintaining a long-term perspective.

2. *The Science of Research: Informed Decision-Making*

- *Fundamental Analysis:* The science of stock market investing involves thorough research and analysis. Fundamental analysis evaluates the financial health of companies, considering factors like earnings, revenue, and growth potential.
- *Technical Analysis:* Technical analysis, another scientific aspect, involves studying price charts and market indicators to identify trends and make

predictions about future price movements.

Investment Strategies: Tailoring Approaches to Individual Goals

1. Long-Term Investing: Planting Seeds for Future Growth

- **Focus on Fundamentals:** Long-term investing centers on the fundamentals of companies. Investors in this category seek stocks with strong financials, sustainable business models, and growth potential over an extended period.
- **Harnessing Compound Interest:** The power of compound interest is a key ally for long-term investors. By reinvesting dividends and allowing investments to grow over time, the compounding effect can significantly boost returns.

2. Day Trading: Navigating the Daily Waves

- **Short-Term Focus:** Day trading represents a more short-term and active approach to stock market investments. Day traders aim to capitalize on intraday price movements, making multiple trades within a single day.
- **Risk and Reward:** While day trading offers the potential for quick profits, it also involves higher risk due to the frequent buying and selling of stocks. Successful day trading requires a keen understanding of market trends and the ability to react swiftly to changing conditions.

Risk Management: The Guardian of Financial Well-Being

1. Diversification: Spreading the Risk

- **Reducing Single-Stock Exposure:** Diversification is a fundamental risk management strategy. Spreading investments across different stocks and sectors helps mitigate the impact of poor performance from a single stock on the overall portfolio.

- **Balancing Risk and Reward:** Diversification aims to balance risk and reward, providing exposure to different market segments and asset classes. This strategy is tailored to protect investors from the potential pitfalls of having all their eggs in one basket.

2. Setting Stop-Loss Orders: A Tactical Shield

- **Automated Risk Mitigation:** Setting stop-loss orders is a tactical approach to risk management. This automated mechanism triggers a sale when a stock reaches a predetermined price, limiting potential losses.
- **Discipline in Action:** Stop-loss orders require discipline, as investors must adhere to predetermined exit points even when faced with emotional responses to market fluctuations.

Embracing Market Volatility: A Test of Resilience

1. The Emotional Rollercoaster of Volatility:

- **Market Corrections and Crashes:** Volatility is an inherent aspect of the stock market. Investors experience emotional highs during market upswings and confront fear and uncertainty during corrections or crashes.
- **Navigating Emotional Responses:** Successfully navigating market volatility involves managing emotional responses. Investors who maintain a disciplined approach and focus on their long-term goals are better positioned to weather market fluctuations.

2. The Contrarian Approach: Harnessing Opportunities in Turbulence

- **Contrarian Investing:** Contrarian investors embrace a counterintuitive approach, often buying stocks when others are selling. This strategy relies on the belief that market sentiments can create opportunities during periods of panic or pessimism.
- **Patience and Conviction:** Contrarian investing requires patience and

conviction in one's analysis. It involves resisting the herd mentality and having confidence in the underlying value of chosen investments.

Mutual funds

In the expansive landscape of personal finance, mutual funds emerge as a cornerstone for individuals seeking a diversified and professionally managed approach to investing. Beyond the technicalities of portfolios and market dynamics, the journey of mutual fund investment is deeply intertwined with human motivations, emotions, and the pursuit of financial well-being.

The Human Element: Motivations and Emotional Landscape

1. Motivations Behind Mutual Fund Investments:

- *Accessibility and Professional Management:* Investors are often drawn to mutual funds for their accessibility and the benefit of professional fund management. Mutual funds provide an avenue for individuals to participate in the financial markets without the need for extensive knowledge or active involvement.
- *Diversification and Risk Mitigation:* The desire for a diversified portfolio and risk mitigation motivates investors to choose mutual funds. The pooled nature of funds allows investors to spread their investments across various securities, reducing exposure to the risks associated with individual stocks

2. Emotional Nuances of Mutual Fund Investing:

- *Trust in Fund Managers:* Investors place a significant level of trust in fund managers to navigate the complexities of the financial markets. The emotional journey involves confidence in the expertise and decision-making capabilities of the professionals managing the mutual fund.

- **Patience Amid Market Fluctuations:** The emotional landscape of mutual fund investing includes the need for patience. Investors may experience a range of emotions during market fluctuations, requiring the resilience to stay committed to their long-term financial goals.

Understanding Mutual Funds: A Human Blend of Simplicity and Complexity

1. The Simplicity of Investing: Mutual Funds as Accessible Portfolios

- **Ease of Entry:** Mutual funds offer a user-friendly entry point into the world of investing. Individuals can start investing with relatively small amounts, making it accessible for those who might be deterred by the complexities of direct stock market participation.
- **Automatic Diversification:** The simplicity of mutual funds lies in their automatic diversification. Investors gain exposure to a diversified portfolio of stocks, bonds, or other securities through a single investment vehicle.

2. The Complexity of Fund Management: Navigating Market Realities

- **Active vs. Passive Management:** Mutual funds may be actively or passively managed, adding a layer of complexity to fund selection. Actively managed funds involve professional fund managers making active investment decisions, while passively managed funds track specific market indices.
- **Market Research and Decision-Making:** The complexity of mutual fund management involves in-depth market research, strategic decision-making, and continuous monitoring of portfolio performance. Fund managers aim to optimize returns within the fund's defined investment objectives.

Investment Strategies: Aligning with Financial Goals

1. Equity Funds: Pursuing Growth with Market Participation

- **Growth-Oriented Goals:** Equity funds appeal to investors with a growth-oriented mindset. These funds predominantly invest in stocks, aiming for capital appreciation over the long term.
- **Risk and Reward Dynamics:** The strategy of equity funds involves a higher level of risk, given the volatility of the stock market. Investors choosing equity funds often do so with an acceptance of short-term market fluctuations for the potential of long-term growth.

2. Debt Funds: Prioritizing Stability and Income Generation

- **Stability and Income Goals:** Debt funds cater to investors seeking stability and regular income. These funds primarily invest in fixed-income securities like government bonds and corporate bonds.
- **Lower Risk, Lower Returns:** The risk associated with debt funds is generally lower compared to equity funds. However, this lower risk profile is often accompanied by relatively lower potential returns.

3. Hybrid Funds: Balancing Growth and Stability

- **Diversified Asset Allocation:** Hybrid funds, also known as balanced funds, maintain a diversified allocation between equity and debt instruments. This strategy aims to balance growth potential with risk mitigation.
- **Adapting to Market Conditions:** Hybrid funds showcase flexibility by adjusting the equity-debt ratio based on market conditions. This adaptability provides a middle ground for investors seeking a blend of growth and stability.

Risk Management: The Guardian of Financial Well-Being

1. Diversification: Spreading Risks Across Asset Classes

- **Reducing Concentration Risk:** Diversification is a fundamental risk man-agement strategy within mutual funds. By spreading investments across different asset classes, such as stocks and bonds, mutual funds aim to reduce the impact of poor performance in any single investment.
- **Creating a Balanced Portfolio:** Diversification within mutual funds creates a balanced portfolio that can weather market volatility and provide a smoother investment experience for individuals.

2. Professional Management: Leveraging Expertise for Risk Mitigation

- **Active Monitoring and Adjustments:** The professional management of mutual funds involves active monitoring of market conditions and making adjustments to the fund's portfolio as needed. Fund managers leverage their expertise to mitigate risks and optimize returns.
- **Risk-Adjusted Returns:** Investors benefit from the risk-adjusted returns provided by mutual fund managers. The expertise and experience of fund managers play a crucial role in navigating the complexities of market risks.

Market Conditions and Investor Psychology

1. Market Downturns: Weathering Storms Through Mutual Funds

- **Collective Resilience:** During market downturns, mutual funds showcase collective resilience. The diversified nature of mutual fund portfolios and the professional management contribute to a level of stability, providing investors with a sense of security amid market turbulence.
- **Emotional Support:** Mutual funds offer emotional support to investors facing market downturns. The professional management and diversi-

fied approach help alleviate the stress associated with individual stock volatility

2. Bull Markets: Riding Waves of Optimism

- **Capitalizing on Growth Opportunities:** In bull markets, mutual funds enable investors to capitalize on growth opportunities. The diversified nature of funds allows investors to participate in the overall upward trajectory of the market.
- **Managing Expectations:** During bull markets, managing expectations becomes crucial. Investors may experience a surge in optimism, and mutual fund managers play a role in tempering expectations while maintaining a focus on long-term goals.

Real estate investments

In the realm of financial endeavors, real estate investments stand as formidable pillars of wealth creation and personal aspirations. Beyond the physical structures and market trends, the journey of real estate investment is deeply human, intertwined with motivations, emotions, and the pursuit of dreams.

The Human Element: Motivations and Emotional Landscape

1. Motivations Behind Real Estate Investments:

- **Homeownership and Stability:** One of the primary motivations for real estate investment is homeownership. Individuals aspire to own a place they can call home, providing a stable foundation for themselves and their families.
- **Wealth Creation and Financial Security:** Beyond the emotional value of a

home, real estate is viewed as a tangible asset that can appreciate over time, creating wealth and offering financial security for the future.

2. Emotional Nuances of Real Estate Investing:

- **Excitement of Ownership:** The journey begins with the excitement of homeownership, whether it's a first home or an additional property. The emotional connection to a place creates a sense of belonging and accomplishment.
- **Challenges and Stress Points:** However, real estate investment comes with its share of challenges, such as property management, market fluctuations, and the financial responsibilities associated with ownership. Navigating these stress points requires emotional resilience and strategic planning.

Understanding Real Estate Investments: A Blend of Dreams and Practicality

1. Residential Real Estate: Homes as Heartfelt Investments

- **Personal Fulfilment:** Purchasing a home that suits one's tastes and lifestyle is frequently the catalyst for residential real estate investments. Living in an environment that fulfills one's identity on an emotional level is a tremendous incentive.
- **Appreciation and Equity Building:** Residential properties can contribute to equity building and appreciation in addition to personal fulfillment. Homeowners enjoy the financial advantages of residential real estate as equity grows with time and as mortgage payments add to the property's worth.

2. Commercial Real Estate: Business Ventures and Financial Gains

- **Entrepreneurial Aspirations:** Commercial real estate investments cater to entrepreneurial spirits seeking to establish businesses or generate rental income. The prospect of creating and managing commercial spaces aligns with aspirations of financial independence and business success.

- **Diversification and Wealth Multiplication:** Commercial properties offer diversification opportunities and the potential for wealth multiplication. The income generated from leases and the appreciation of commercial assets contribute to a robust financial portfolio.

Investment Strategies: Tailoring Approaches to Individual Goals

1. Buy and Hold Strategy: Cultivating Long-Term Wealth

- **Long-Term Wealth Accumulation:** The buy and hold strategy involves acquiring properties with the intention of holding them for an extended period. This approach aligns with the goal of long-term wealth accumulation through property appreciation and rental income.
- **Patience as a Virtue:** Successful execution of the buy and hold strategy requires patience. Investors must weather market fluctuations and economic cycles while maintaining a focus on the long-term growth potential of their real estate holdings.

2. Fix and Flip Strategy: Capitalizing on Short-Term Opportunities

- **Short-Term Profit Maximization:** The fix and flip strategy revolves around acquiring properties in need of renovation, improving them, and selling for a profit. Investors are drawn to the potential for quick returns and the satisfaction of transforming distressed properties.
- **Market Timing and Skill:** Success in fix and flip investing involves adept market timing and renovation skills. Investors must accurately assess the market conditions, estimate renovation costs, and execute the improvements effectively to maximize profits.

Risk Management: Navigating the Terrain of Property Ownership

1. *Market Research and Due Diligence: The Guardian of Property Investments*

- *Informed Decision-Making:* Market research and due diligence play a pivotal role in risk management for real estate investors. Informed decision-making involves evaluating property values, analyzing market trends, and understanding the potential risks and rewards associated with a specific location.
- *Mitigating Unforeseen Challenges:* Thorough research equips investors to anticipate and mitigate unforeseen challenges, ensuring that their real estate ventures align with their financial goals

2. *Property Management: The Operational Shield*

- *Effective Property Management:* Successful real estate investment requires effective property management. Whether it's a residential property or a commercial space, diligent management ensures that the property remains well-maintained, attractive to tenants, and positioned for long-term value appreciation.
- *Outsourcing for Efficiency:* Investors may choose to outsource property management tasks to professionals, reducing the burden of day-to-day operations. This allows investors to focus on strategic decision-making rather than getting bogged down by operational details.

Market Conditions and Investor Psychology

1. *Market Upswings: Capitalizing on Appreciation*

- *Optimism and Opportunities:* During market upswings, real estate investors experience optimism and see opportunities for property appreciation. The potential for higher property values and increased demand creates a favorable environment for buying, selling, or holding properties.

· **Strategic Decision-Making:** Investors must balance optimism with strategic decision-making. The timing of buying or selling properties during market upswings requires careful consideration to maximize returns.

2. *Market Downturns: Navigating Challenges with Resilience*

· **Adaptability and Resilience:** Market downturns pose challenges for real estate investors. Economic recessions or fluctuations in demand can impact property values and rental income. Adaptability and resilience become essential qualities for investors navigating these challenging periods.

· **Identifying Bargains and Bargaining Power:** However, market downturns also present opportunities. Savvy investors may identify undervalued properties and negotiate favorable deals during these times, leveraging their bargaining power

6

Chapter Five: Retirement Planning

Importance of retirement planning

Among the many factors to consider when making financial decisions, retirement planning stands out as crucial for individuals who want to plan their golden years with confidence and financial stability. The process of planning for retirement is very personal, involving goals, feelings, and the innate desire for a happy life after work. It goes beyond figures and investment portfolios.

The Human Element: Motivations and Emotional Landscape

1. *Motivations Behind Retirement Planning: Crafting the Future You Envision*

- *Financial Independence:* At the heart of retirement planning lies the aspiration for financial independence. Individuals seek to secure a future where they can maintain their lifestyle, meet healthcare needs, and pursue personal interests without being tethered to employment.
- *Legacy and Family Well-Being:* Beyond personal needs, many embark on retirement planning with the desire to leave a legacy and ensure the well-being of their families. It becomes a journey of not just self-sufficiency

but also the provision of support and comfort for loved ones.

2. *Emotional Nuances of Retirement Planning: Balancing Aspirations and Realities*

- *Anticipation of Freedom:* The journey begins with the anticipation of freedom – freedom from work obligations and the opportunity to embrace a more leisurely pace of life. This phase is often marked by excitement about the potential for travel, pursuing hobbies, and spending quality time with loved ones.
- *Concerns and Anxieties:* However, retirement planning is not devoid of concerns and anxieties. Individuals grapple with questions about whether their savings will be sufficient, how to navigate healthcare costs, and the emotional adjustment to a shift in daily routines. Balancing these concerns requires a delicate interplay of financial prudence and emotional resilience.

Understanding Retirement Planning: A Symphony of Financial Well-Being

1. *Savings and Investments: Building the Financial Foundation*

- *Early Start for Long-Term Growth:* The importance of starting retirement planning early cannot be overstated. Time becomes a valuable ally in the pursuit of long-term growth through compounding. Individuals who begin saving for retirement in their early working years have the advantage of letting their investments grow over decades.
- *Strategic Asset Allocation:* Retirement planning involves strategic asset allocation, balancing risk and return based on individual goals, risk tolerance, and time horizon. This careful calibration ensures that the portfolio is aligned with the financial objectives of the retiree

2. *Pensions and Social Security: Pillars of Financial Support*

- **Pensions:** *A Traditional Safeguard:* Pensions, although less prevalent in modern employment structures, remain a vital component of retirement planning for some individuals. Pensions offer a predictable source of income, often linked to the individual's years of service and salary history.
- **Social Security:** *A Social Safety Net:* Social Security serves as a social safety net, providing a foundation of income for retirees. Understanding the nuances of Social Security benefits, including when to claim them, becomes an integral aspect of retirement planning strategy.

Investment Strategies: Personalizing Approaches for Life After Work

1. *Conservative vs. Aggressive Investment Strategies: Aligning with Risk Tolerance*

- **Conservative Approach:** Some retirees lean towards a conservative investment strategy, prioritizing capital preservation and a steady income stream. This approach often involves a higher allocation to fixed-income investments, such as bonds and certificates of deposit, to minimize market volatility.
- **Aggressive Approach:** Conversely, others adopt a more aggressive approach, maintaining a higher allocation to equities to harness the potential for long-term growth. This strategy requires a higher tolerance for market fluctuations but aims to capitalize on the potential for increased returns.

2. *Diversification: Guarding Against Market Volatility*

- **Spreading Risk Across Assets:** Diversification remains a key tenet of retirement planning. Spreading investments across a diverse range of asset classes, including stocks, bonds, and real estate, guards against the impact of poor performance in any single investment.
- **Balancing Growth and Stability:** The goal is to strike a balance between

growth and stability. Diversification helps retirees manage risk while seeking opportunities for their portfolio to grow over time.

Risk Management: Safeguarding Financial Well-Being in Retirement

1. Longevity Risk: Planning for a Lengthy Retirement

- *Advancements in Longevity:* With advancements in healthcare and improvements in living standards, retirees face the prospect of longer life expectancies. Longevity risk the risk of outliving one's savings necessitates careful planning to ensure financial resources align with the duration of retirement.
- *Strategies for Long-Term Sustainability:* Strategies to mitigate longevity risk include optimizing Social Security benefits, incorporating annuities for guaranteed income, and regularly reassessing withdrawal rates to ensure financial sustainability throughout retirement.

2. Healthcare Costs: Navigating the Complex Terrain

- **Rising Healthcare Expenses:** Healthcare costs represent a significant consideration in retirement planning. As individuals age, the potential for increased medical expenses becomes a reality. Retirees must factor in the costs of insurance premiums, prescription medications, and potential long-term care needs.
- **Health Savings Accounts (HSAs) and Medicare Planning:** Leveraging Health Savings Accounts (HSAs) and understanding the nuances of Medicare become critical components of retirement planning. Strategic planning for healthcare costs involves anticipating needs and exploring insurance options that align with individual circumstances.

Emotional Well-Being in Retirement: The Human Fulfillment Factor

1. Psychological Transition: Shifting from Work to Leisure

- **Identity and Purpose:** Retirement marks a profound psychological transition, often requiring individuals to redefine their sense of identity and purpose. Many derive a significant portion of their identity from their professional roles, and the shift to retirement prompts introspection about how to find purpose and fulfillment outside of work.
- **The Pursuit of Hobbies and Passions:** Retirement planning extends beyond financial considerations to encompass the pursuit of hobbies and passions. The ability to dedicate time to activities that bring joy and fulfillment becomes a crucial aspect of emotional well-being in retirement.

2. Social Connections: Building a Supportive Network

- **Community and Relationships:** Social connections play a pivotal role in the emotional landscape of retirement. Retirees often find fulfillment in community involvement, building relationships with peers, and participating in social activities. A supportive network contributes to a sense of belonging and combats potential feelings of isolation.
- **Family Dynamics and Support Systems:** Family dynamics also come into focus during retirement. Maintaining open communication and aligning expectations with family members contribute to a supportive environment where emotional well-being is nurtured.

401(k), IRAs, and other retirement accounts

While choosing the appropriate retirement funds, individuals have a plethora of options to consider within the complex framework of retirement planning. One cannot stress how crucial it is to develop a customised plan that is based on a knowledge of each person's preferences and aspirations.

The Human Element: Motivations and Emotional Landscape

1. Motivations Behind Retirement Accounts:

- **Financial Independence and Security:** At the core of retirement accounts lies the motivation for financial independence and security. Individuals seek instruments that will allow them to enjoy their golden years with a sense of financial assurance, free from the constraints of employment.
- **Tailoring to Individual Aspirations:** The desire for customization is a humanizing element in retirement planning. Different individuals have unique aspirations, and retirement accounts offer a canvas for tailoring financial strategies to align with those dreams.

2. Emotional Nuances of Retirement Account Selection:

- **Hope and Optimism:** The selection of retirement accounts often begins with hope and optimism. Individuals envision a future where their diligent savings efforts culminate in a comfortable retirement. The emotional landscape is marked by the anticipation of realizing long-held dreams.
- **Decision-Anxiety and Prudent Choices:** Simultaneously, the process involves decision-anxiety as individuals navigate the myriad options. Making prudent choices requires a careful evaluation of risk tolerance, time horizons, and an awareness of the emotional aspects associated with each retirement account.

Understanding Retirement Accounts:

1. 401(k): The Workplace Maestro

- **Employer-Sponsored Advantage:** The 401(k) plan stands as a workplace maestro, offering employees an employer-sponsored avenue for retirement savings. The allure lies in the potential for employer matching contributions, which can significantly boost the overall retirement nest egg.
- **Employee Contributions and Tax Benefits:** Employees contribute to their 401(k) accounts through salary deferrals, enjoying the dual benefit of reducing taxable income and allowing their contributions to grow tax-deferred until withdrawal during retirement

2. IRAs (Traditional and Roth): Personalized Crescendos

- **Traditional IRA: The Tax-Deferred Sonata:** The Traditional IRA provides a tax-deferred sonata, allowing individuals to make contributions with pre-tax dollars. While contributions reduce taxable income, taxes are deferred until withdrawals during retirement. This option is favored by those anticipating a lower tax bracket in retirement.
- **Roth IRA: The Tax-Free Melody:** The Roth IRA, on the other hand, introduces a tax-free melody. Contributions are made with after-tax dollars, but withdrawals, including investment gains, are tax-free during retirement. Roth IRAs are favored by those anticipating higher tax brackets in retirement or valuing tax diversification.

2. Other Retirement Accounts: Diversifying Harmonies

- **SEP-IRA and SIMPLE IRA: Small Business Serenades:** For small business owners and the self-employed, SEP-IRAs and SIMPLE IRAs offer harmonies of simplicity and tax advantages. These plans provide avenues for both employer and employee contributions, allowing businesses to tailor retirement benefits to their unique circumstances.

- *Solo 401(k): A Solo Performance:* The Solo 401(k) serves as a solo perfor-mance for self-employed individuals or small business owners with no employees (except a spouse). This plan combines elements of a traditional 401(k) with additional features for self-employed professionals.

Investment Strategies: Crafting Melodies for Retirement Goals

1. Asset Allocation: The Musical Composition of Portfolios

- *Balancing Risk and Return:* The art of retirement planning involves crafting a musical composition of asset allocation. Individuals must balance risk and return, aligning investments with their risk tolerance, time horizon, and overall retirement goals.
- *Diversification: The Harmony of Risk Mitigation:* Diversification emerges as a harmonious element, spreading investments across different asset classes to mitigate risk. Retirement accounts become the instruments through which individuals orchestrate a well-diversified portfolio.

Lifecycle Funds: A Symphony of Automatic Adjustments

- *Target-Date Funds: Adapting to Life's Stages:* Lifecycle funds, particularly target-date funds, offer a symphony of automatic adjustments based on an individual's anticipated retirement date. These funds automati-cally shift asset allocations over time, becoming more conservative as retirement approaches.
- *Set-and-Forget Simplicity:* Target-date funds provide simplicity for those who prefer a set-and-forget approach. Investors choose a fund with a target retirement date closest to their own, and the fund manager handles the rest, adjusting allocations to align with the chosen retirement horizon.

Risk Management: Safeguarding Melodies in Retirement Planning

1. Monitoring and Rebalancing: The Conductor's Baton

- **Regular Portfolio Check-Ups:** The conductor's baton in retirement planning involves regular monitoring and rebalancing. Individuals need to conduct periodic check-ups on their portfolios, ensuring that the asset allocation aligns with their risk tolerance and goals.
- **Adapting to Market Changes:** The ability to adapt to market changes becomes crucial. Periodic rebalancing allows investors to realign their portfolios, taking advantage of growth opportunities while mitigating risks during market fluctuations.

2. Emergency Funds: The Financial Safety Net Symphony

- **Buffering Against Unexpected Challenges:** Like a safety net symphony, emergency funds play a crucial role in retirement planning. These funds act as a financial buffer, providing a safety net against unexpected challenges such as medical emergencies, home repairs, or other unforeseen expenses.
- **Preserving Retirement Accounts:** Having an emergency fund safeguards retirement accounts from premature withdrawals, preserving the intended purpose of these funds for retirement income.

Market Conditions and Investor Psychology: The Human Tempo in Retirement Planning

1. Market Volatility: The Symphony of Resilience

- **Navigating the Peaks and Valleys:** Market volatility introduces peaks and valleys in the retirement planning symphony. Individuals must navigate these fluctuations with resilience, understanding that short-term market movements are part of the broader, long-term retirement composition.

- **Emotional Fortitude:** Developing emotional fortitude becomes crucial during times of market uncertainty. Retirees and pre-retirees alike must resist impulsive decisions driven by short-term market movements and maintain a focus on long-term objectives.

2. Life Changes: Adapting the Melody to New Chapters

- **Adapting to Transitions:** Life changes, whether planned or unexpected, prompt individuals to adapt the melody of retirement planning. These transitions may include relocation, changes in family dynamics, or shifts in health. Flexibility and a willingness to recalibrate retirement strategies become essential.
- **Financial Advisors as Conductors:** Financial advisors serve as conductors, guiding individuals through life's transitions. Their expertise helps individuals adjust their retirement plans in response to changing circumstances, ensuring that the financial composition remains harmonious.

7

Chapter Six: Risk Management

Insurance considerations

In the tapestry of financial planning, insurance serves as a critical thread, weaving a safety net to protect against unforeseen challenges. Beyond the numbers and policies, the realm of insurance considerations is deeply human, reflecting aspirations, fears, and the innate desire to safeguard what matters most.

The Human Element: Motivations and Emotional Landscape

1. Motivations Behind Insurance: Shielding Dreams and Loved Ones

- **Protection of Loved Ones:** At the core of insurance motivations lies the instinct to protect loved ones. Individuals seek insurance coverage to ensure financial stability for their families in the event of unforeseen circumstances, such as illness, accidents, or premature death.
- **Safeguarding Dreams and Aspirations:** Insurance is not merely a financial instrument but a guardian of dreams and aspirations. It serves as a safety net, allowing individuals to pursue their goals with the reassurance that their financial foundation is secure.

2. Emotional Nuances of Insurance Planning: Balancing Prudence and Peace of Mind

- **Anticipation of the Unexpected:** Insurance planning begins with the anticipation of the unexpected. Individuals grapple with the uncertainty of life's twists and turns, recognizing the need to prepare for scenarios that may impact their health, property, or financial well-being.
- **Peace of Mind and Emotional Resilience:** The emotional landscape involves seeking peace of mind through insurance. Knowing that there is a safety net in place provides a sense of security and emotional resilience, allowing individuals to navigate challenges with greater confidence.

Understanding Insurance: A Symphony of Protection

1. Life Insurance: Orchestrating Financial Security for Loved Ones

- **Term Life Insurance: A Temporary Crescendo:** Term life insurance acts as a temporary crescendo, providing coverage for a specific term. It is often chosen to protect financial responsibilities such as mortgage payments, education expenses, or income replacement during the working years.
- **Whole Life Insurance: A Lifelong Melody:** Whole life insurance, on the other hand, offers a lifelong melody. It provides coverage until the policyholder's death and includes a cash value component that grows over time. Whole life insurance can serve both as protection and an investment vehicle.

2. Health Insurance: Harmonizing Wellness and Financial Security

- **Coverage for Medical Expenses:** Health insurance plays a vital role in harmonizing wellness and financial security. It provides coverage for medical expenses, including doctor visits, hospital stays, and prescription medications. Health insurance ensures that individuals can access necessary healthcare without facing crippling financial burdens.

- **Preventive Care and Well-Being:** Beyond reactive coverage, health insurance encourages preventive care and well-being. Routine check-ups, vaccinations, and screenings contribute to early detection of potential health issues, fostering a proactive approach to overall well-being.

3. Property Insurance: Protecting Homes and Valuables

- **Homeowner's Insurance: A Shield for Residences:** Homeowner's insurance acts as a shield for residences, offering coverage for damages or losses due to perils such as fire, theft, or natural disasters. It not only protects the structure of the home but also covers personal belongings within.
- **Renters Insurance: Safeguarding Possessions:** Renters insurance provides a similar shield for individuals renting homes or apartments. It safeguards personal possessions against covered perils, offering a layer of financial protection for tenants.

4. Auto Insurance: Navigating the Roads of Financial Security

- **Liability Coverage: Protecting Against Accidents:** Auto insurance navigates the roads of financial security by providing liability coverage. This protects individuals against financial responsibility for injuries or property damage caused to others in accidents for which they are at fault.
- **Comprehensive and Collision Coverage: Safeguarding the Vehicle:** Comprehensive and collision coverage safeguard the vehicle itself. These components of auto insurance provide protection against damages resulting from events such as theft, vandalism, or collisions with objects.

Investment Strategies: Insurance as a Pillar of Financial Planning

1. Integration of Insurance with Investment Portfolios: A Harmonious Ensemble

- **Balancing Risk and Protection:** The integration of insurance with investment portfolios forms a harmonious ensemble in financial planning.

Balancing risk and protection involves assessing the level of coverage needed to safeguard against potential financial setbacks while optimizing investment strategies for long-term growth.

· **Diversification Beyond Investments:** Diversification extends beyond investment portfolios to include insurance considerations. This holistic approach ensures that individuals have a well-rounded financial strategy that addresses both market risks and unforeseen life events.

2. Annuities: Orchestrating Lifetime Income Streams

· **Fixed Annuities: The Melody of Guaranteed Income:** Fixed annuities offer the melody of guaranteed income. Individuals invest a lump sum, and in return, receive regular payments for a predetermined period or even for life. Fixed annuities provide a stable source of income, acting as a complement to retirement planning.

· **Variable Annuities: Navigating Market-Linked Tunes:** Variable annuities navigate market-linked tunes. These instruments allow individuals to invest in a variety of sub-accounts, providing the potential for higher returns. Variable annuities often include features such as death benefits and optional riders for added flexibility.

Risk Management: Symphony of Financial Protection

1. Assessing Risk Tolerance: The Conductor's Baton in Insurance Planning

· **Personalized Risk Evaluation:** Assessing risk tolerance becomes the conductor's baton in insurance planning. Individuals must conduct a personalized evaluation of their risk tolerance, considering factors such as financial goals, family dynamics, and comfort with uncertainty.

· **Aligning Coverage with Life Stages:** The orchestration involves aligning insurance coverage with different life stages. Young families may prioritize life and health insurance for income protection, while retirees may focus on maintaining adequate coverage for medical expenses and property protection.

2. Emergency Funds: The Financial Safety Net Symphony Revisited

- **Linking Insurance to Emergency Preparedness:** Emergency funds and insurance form a collaborative symphony in financial safety. Linking insurance to emergency preparedness involves ensuring that coverage aligns with potential risks, creating a comprehensive safety net for unexpected challenges.
- **Preserving Financial Stability:** The goal is to preserve financial stability during unforeseen events. Insurance, in conjunction with emergency funds, acts as a buffer, allowing individuals and families to weather storms without compromising long-term financial goals.

Market Conditions and Investor Psychology: The Human Tempo in Insurance Planning

1. Market Fluctuations: Maintaining Harmony Amidst Uncertainty

- **Navigating Premium Adjustments:** Market fluctuations impact insurance premiums, requiring individuals to navigate adjustments in coverage costs. The ability to adapt to changing premium rates involves a thoughtful reassessment of coverage needs and potential cost-saving strategies.
- **Insurance as a Long-Term Strategy:** Understanding insurance as a long-term strategy becomes crucial during market uncertainties. While short-term fluctuations may influence premium costs, insurance serves as a steady pillar in a comprehensive financial plan, providing stability over the years.

2. Life Changes: Adapting the Melody to New Chapters

- **Adjusting Coverage with Life Milestones:** Life changes prompt individuals to adapt the melody of insurance planning. Marriage, childbirth, home purchases, or career shifts may necessitate adjustments in coverage. Flexibility in insurance planning allows individuals to seamlessly adapt their policies to new chapters in life.

- **Reviewing Policies Periodically:** Periodic reviews of insurance policies ensure that coverage remains aligned with evolving life circumstances. Whether celebrating milestones or navigating challenges, adapting the insurance melody to new chapters contributes to a resilient and comprehensive financial plan.

Hedging strategies

In the intricate dance of financial markets, uncertainty is a constant partner. In response to the ebb and flow of economic landscapes, individuals and businesses seek strategies to protect against adverse movements and minimize risks. Hedging strategies emerge as a vital tool in this symphony of financial planning, offering a nuanced approach to safeguarding assets and investments.

The Human Element: Motivations and Emotional Landscape

1. Motivations Behind Hedging: Preserving Financial Foundations

- **Fear of Adverse Movements:** At the heart of hedging motivations lies the fear of adverse movements in financial markets. Individuals and businesses alike harbor concerns about the impact of volatility on their assets and investments. Hedging serves as a shield against these uncertainties, preserving financial foundations.
- **Protecting Against Downside Risks:** The emotional landscape involves a desire to protect against downside risks. Hedging strategies provide a sense of security, allowing individuals and businesses to navigate market fluctuations without the fear of catastrophic financial losses.

2. Emotional Nuances of Hedging: Balancing Caution and Opportunity

- **Caution in Uncertain Times:** Hedging is often associated with caution, especially in uncertain economic climates. The emotional nuances include a prudent approach to financial decision-making, acknowledging that markets can be unpredictable, and embracing strategies to mitigate potential downsides.
- **Seizing Opportunities Amidst Protection:** Interestingly, hedging strategies also involve seizing opportunities amidst protection. The emotional landscape encompasses a balanced perspective – while guarding against risks, individuals and businesses aim to position themselves to capitalize on market opportunities that may arise.

Understanding Hedging: A Symphony of Risk Management

1. Derivatives: Orchestrating Protection Through Financial Instruments

- **Futures Contracts: A Forward Melody:** Futures contracts act as a forward melody in hedging strategies. These financial instruments allow parties to lock in prices for future transactions, providing protection against adverse price movements in commodities, currencies, or financial assets.
- **Options Contracts: The Harmonic Balance:** Options contracts introduce a harmonic balance. They provide the buyer with the right, but not the obligation, to buy (call option) or sell (put option) an asset at a predetermined price. Options offer flexibility in hedging strategies, allowing participants to tailor their risk exposure.

2. Forwards and Swaps: Navigating the Seas of Market Risks

- **Forward Contracts: Sailing Towards Price Certainty:** Forward contracts involve sailing towards price certainty. Similar to futures, these agreements allow parties to lock in future prices. While forwards are customizable and traded over the counter, they lack the standardized features of exchange-traded futures.

- **Interest Rate Swaps:** *Calibrating Interest Rate Harmonies:* Interest rate swaps calibrate harmonies in hedging interest rate risks. These agreements involve the exchange of cash flows between parties with differing interest rate exposures. Swaps provide a tool for managing interest rate fluctuations in loans, bonds, or other financial instruments.

Investment Strategies: Hedging as a Risk Mitigation Instrument

1. Balancing Act: Integrating Hedging with Investment Portfolios

- **Diversification and Hedging:** *A Synchronised Ballet:* Hedging is integrated with investment portfolios in a synchronized ballet. Diversification and hedging work together to form a balanced investing strategy. While diversification spreads risk across multiple assets, hedging adds an extra layer of protection against certain dangers.

2. Currency Hedging: Navigating Forex Seas with Stability

- **Foreign exchange risks:** *A choppy sea of uncertainty:* Currency hedging helps individuals manage the stormy waters of foreign exchange risk. Currency fluctuations can have an influence on profitability for businesses that deal internationally. Currency hedging measures, such as forward contracts and currency options, offer stability in unpredictable forex markets.

Risk Management: Safeguarding Melodies in Financial Planning

1. Assessing Risk Tolerance: The Conductor's Baton in Hedging Strategies

- **Personalized Risk Evaluation:** Assessing risk tolerance becomes the conductor's baton in insurance planning. Individuals must conduct a personalized evaluation of their risk tolerance, considering factors such as financial goals, family dynamics, and comfort with uncertainty.

- *Aligning Coverage with Life Stages:* The orchestration involves aligning insurance coverage with different life stages. Young families may prioritize life and health insurance for income protection, while retirees may focus on maintaining adequate coverage for medical expenses and property protection.

2. Emergency Funds: The Financial Safety Net Symphony Revisited

- *Linking Insurance to Emergency Preparedness:* Emergency funds and insurance form a collaborative symphony in financial safety. Linking insurance to emergency preparedness involves ensuring that coverage aligns with potential risks, creating a comprehensive safety net for unexpected challenges.
- *Preserving Financial Stability:* The goal is to preserve financial stability during unforeseen events. Insurance, in conjunction with emergency funds, acts as a buffer, allowing individuals and families to weather storms without compromising long-term financial goals.

Market Conditions and Investor Psychology: The Human Tempo in Insurance Planning

1. Market Fluctuations: Maintaining Harmony Amidst Uncertainty

- *Navigating Premium Adjustments:* Market fluctuations impact insurance premiums, requiring individuals to navigate adjustments in coverage costs. The ability to adapt to changing premium rates involves a thoughtful reassessment of coverage needs and potential cost-saving strategies.
- *Insurance as a Long-Term Strategy:* Understanding insurance as a long-term strategy becomes crucial during market uncertainties. While short-term fluctuations may influence premium costs, insurance serves as a steady pillar in a comprehensive financial plan, providing stability over the years.

2. *Life Changes: Adapting the Melody to New Chapters*

- *Adjusting Coverage with Life Milestones:* Life changes prompt individuals to adapt the melody of insurance planning. Marriage, childbirth, home purchases, or career shifts may necessitate adjustments in coverage. Flexibility in insurance planning allows individuals to seamlessly adapt their policies to new chapters in life.
- *Reviewing Policies Periodically:* Periodic reviews of insurance policies ensure that coverage remains aligned with evolving life circumstances. Whether celebrating milestones or navigating challenges, adapting the insurance melody to new chapters contributes to a resilient and comprehensive financial plan.

8

Chapter Seven: Monitoring and Adjusting Your Portfolio

Regularly reviewing investments

I n the ever-evolving landscape of finance, the importance of regularly reviewing investments cannot be overstated. Like a skilled conductor leading an orchestra, investors must orchestrate a harmonious blend of vigilance, strategy, and adaptability to ensure their financial symphony plays out according to plan.

The Human Element: Motivations and Emotional Landscape

1. Motivations Behind Regular Review: Nurturing Financial Wellness

- **Aspirations and Goals:** Regularly reviewing investments is motivated by the desire to nurture financial wellness. Investors embark on this journey with specific aspirations and goals – be it funding a child's education, purchasing a home, or enjoying a comfortable retirement. The emotional landscape involves a commitment to realizing these financial dreams.
- **Fear of Uncertainty:** Fear of uncertainty is a powerful motivator. Investors

recognize that financial markets are dynamic and subject to fluctuations. Regular reviews serve as a shield against the unknown, providing a sense of control and assurance in the face of market volatility.

2. *Emotional Nuances of Investment Reviews: Balancing Caution and Optimism*

- **Caution in Changing Times:** Investment reviews often involve a sense of caution, especially during changing economic climates. The emotional nuances include a prudent approach to assessing risks and returns, acknowledging that market conditions can shift, impacting the performance of investments.
- **Optimism and Growth Potential:** Conversely, investment reviews are infused with optimism. Investors review their portfolios not only to identify potential risks but also to uncover growth opportunities. The emotional landscape includes a belief in the potential for financial growth through strategic adjustments.

Understanding Regular Investment Reviews: A Symphony of Financial Insight

1. *Monitoring Asset Allocation: Maintaining a Harmonious Composition*

- **Balancing Risk and Return:** The art of regularly reviewing investments begins with monitoring asset allocation. Investors aim to balance risk and return by assessing how their assets are distributed across various classes such as stocks, bonds, and cash. The goal is to ensure that the portfolio aligns with their risk tolerance and financial objectives.
- **Adapting to Market Conditions:** Regular reviews involve adapting to changing market conditions. Asset allocation strategies may need adjustment based on economic trends, interest rate movements, and geopolitical events. Investors act as vigilant conductors, making fine-tuned changes to maintain a harmonious investment composition.

2. *Performance Evaluation: Assessing the Crescendos and Diminuendos*

- **Tracking Returns and Losses:** Performance evaluation is akin to assessing the crescendos and diminuendos in a musical composition. Investors meticulously track returns and losses across their investment portfolio. This process involves comparing performance against benchmarks, goals, and expectations set during the initial investment strategy.
- **Learning from Mistakes:** A humanized approach to performance evaluation includes learning from mistakes. Investors acknowledge that not every investment decision will yield positive results. Regular reviews provide opportunities to reflect on missteps, refine strategies, and cultivate a resilient and informed investment mindset.

Investment Strategies: Adapting Melodies for Long-Term Goals

1. *Adjusting Strategies for Life's Movements: A Dynamic Sonata*

- **Aligning with Life Changes:** Investment strategies are not static; they evolve like the movements in a sonata. Regularly reviewing investments involves aligning strategies with life changes. Whether it's a career move, marriage, or the birth of a child, investors adapt their portfolios to reflect new priorities and timelines.
- **Flexibility as a Virtue:** Flexibility emerges as a virtue in adapting investment strategies. Regular reviews enable investors to remain nimble, adjusting their approach to navigate the ever-changing dynamics of financial markets and personal circumstances.

2. *Tax-Efficient Investing: Orchestrating Financial Harmony*

- *Optimizing Tax Efficiency:* Tax considerations play a crucial role in orchestrating financial harmony. Investors aim to optimize tax efficiency by regularly reviewing their portfolios for tax implications. This involves assessing capital gains, harvesting tax losses, and exploring tax-advantaged investment vehicles.

- *Strategic Tax Planning:* Strategic tax planning becomes part of the investment symphony. Investors may adjust their portfolios to minimize tax liabilities, maximize deductions, and capitalize on tax-efficient investment strategies. This proactive approach aligns with the broader goal of preserving and growing wealth.

Risk Management: Safeguarding Melodies in Investment Reviews

1. Monitoring Risks: The Conductor's Baton in Investment Symphony

- **Identifying Potential Risks:** Monitoring risks is akin to wielding the conductor's baton in the investment symphony. Regular reviews involve identifying potential risks that may impact the portfolio's performance. This includes market risks, sector-specific risks, and external factors that could influence investment outcomes.
- **Conducting Stress Tests:** Stress testing the portfolio becomes a crucial aspect of risk management. Investors simulate various scenarios to assess how their investments would fare under adverse conditions. This proactive approach ensures a resilient investment composition that can withstand unexpected challenges.

2. Emergency Funds: The Financial Safety Net Symphony Revisited

- **Linking Investment Reviews to Emergency Preparedness:** Investment reviews and emergency funds form a collaborative symphony in financial safety. Linking investment reviews to emergency preparedness involves recognizing that unforeseen events can impact both the investment portfolio and overall financial stability. Maintaining emergency funds ensures a safety net during turbulent market periods.

Market Conditions and Investor Psychology: The Human Tempo in Investment Reviews

1. Navigating Market Volatility: A Symphony of Resilience

- **Embracing the Rhythm of Market Fluctuations:** Navigating market volatility is a symphony of resilience. Investors acknowledge that market fluctuations are part of the rhythm in the financial landscape. Regular investment reviews involve embracing this rhythm, and understanding that short-term market movements should not overshadow long-term investment goals.
- **Emotional Fortitude:** Developing emotional fortitude becomes crucial during times of market uncertainty. Investors must resist impulsive decisions driven by short-term market movements and maintain a focus on long-term objectives. Emotional fortitude ensures a steady tempo in the face of market fluctuations.

2. Life Changes: Adapting the Melody to New Chapters

- **Adjusting Portfolios with Life Transitions:** Life changes prompt investors to adapt the melody of their investment strategy. Whether entering retirement, facing health challenges, or experiencing a major life event, individuals adjust their portfolios to align with new chapters. Flexibility and a willingness to recalibrate investment strategies contribute to a resilient and comprehensive financial plan.

Making informed adjustments

In the intricate dance of financial planning, making informed adjustments to your investment portfolio is akin to refining the notes in a beautiful symphony. Just as a skilled conductor fine-tunes the orchestra for a flawless performance, investors must delicately adjust their portfolios to achieve a harmonious blend of risk management, growth, and adaptability.

The Human Element: Motivations and Emotional Landscape

1. Motivations Behind Informed Adjustments: Nurturing Financial Well-Being

- **Alignment with Financial Goals:** Making informed adjustments is motivated by the deep-rooted desire to nurture financial well-being. Investors embark on this journey to align their portfolios with specific financial goals be it buying a home, funding education, or securing a comfortable retirement. The emotional landscape involves a commitment to realizing these aspirations.
- **Adapting to Life Changes:** Life is dynamic, and so are the motivations behind informed adjustments. Investors recognize that life changes from career shifts to family milestones necessitate adaptations in their financial strategy. The emotional nuances include a willingness to adjust and thrive amidst the evolving rhythm of life.

2. Emotional Nuances of Adjustment: Balancing Caution and Optimism

- **Prudence in Market Volatility:** Adjusting a portfolio often involves a sense of prudence, especially during periods of market volatility. The emotional nuances include a cautious approach to assessing risks and returns, acknowledging that markets can be unpredictable and require careful navigation.
- **Optimism for Future Growth:** Contrarily, making informed adjustments is infused with optimism. Investors undertake these refinements not only to mitigate risks but also to position themselves for future growth. The emotional landscape encompasses a belief in the potential for positive outcomes through strategic and well-informed adjustments.

Understanding Informed Adjustments: A Symphony of Financial Insight

1. Strategic Reallocation: Tuning the Asset Composition for Harmony

- **Assessing Risk Tolerance:** Making informed adjustments often begins with assessing risk tolerance. Investors fine-tune their asset allocation to strike a balance between risk and return. This strategic reallocation ensures that the portfolio aligns with their risk preferences and long-term financial objectives.
- **Adapting to Economic Trends:** The art of making informed adjustments involves adapting to changing economic trends. Investors must be attuned to shifts in interest rates, market conditions, and global economic factors. By making adjustments in response to these trends, they maintain a harmonious investment composition.

2. Optimizing for Tax Efficiency: Crafting a Melody of Financial Advantage

- **Tax-Loss Harvesting: A Tactical Tune-Up:** Informed adjustments often include optimizing for tax efficiency. Tax-loss harvesting is a tactical tune-up that involves selling investments at a loss to offset gains and reduce tax liabilities. Investors orchestrate this process to create a tax-efficient melody within their portfolios.
- **Strategic Capital Gains Management: Harmonizing Tax Implications:** Strategic capital gains management becomes part of the symphony. Investors carefully time the realization of capital gains to align with their overall tax strategy. This harmonizing of tax implications ensures that adjustments contribute to the financial advantage of the portfolio.

Investment Strategies: Crafting a Sonata of Growth and Stability

1. Evaluating Underperforming Assets: Reshaping the Musical Landscape

- **Reflecting on Performance:** Making informed adjustments involves evaluating underperforming assets to reshape the musical landscape. Investors reflect on the performance of individual investments, considering factors such as market conditions, company fundamentals, and external influences. This introspection guides decisions on whether to retain, adjust, or divest from specific holdings.
- **Cultivating a Resilient Mindset:** A humanized approach to evaluating underperforming assets includes cultivating a resilient mindset. Investors recognize that not every investment decision will yield positive results. Informed adjustments provide an opportunity for introspection, learning from setbacks, and refining strategies for future growth.

2. Aligning with Long-Term Goals: A Harmonious Composition

- **Dynamic Asset Allocation: Responding to Changing Goals:** Informed adjustments are a dynamic process that involves aligning the portfolio with long-term goals. As life unfolds, goals may shift, and investors respond by dynamically adjusting asset allocation. Whether the goal is wealth accumulation, income generation, or capital preservation, the composition of the portfolio evolves to create a harmonious financial composition.
- **Balancing Growth and Stability:** A Sonata of Financial Resilience: Balancing growth and stability becomes a key theme in the symphony of informed adjustments. Investors carefully craft a sonata that incorporates growth-oriented assets for wealth appreciation and stability-focused assets to weather market uncertainties. This balanced approach ensures a resilient and adaptive financial composition.

Risk Management: Safeguarding Melodies in Adjustment Strategies

1. Stress Testing: Evaluating the Resilience of Financial Compositions

- **Simulating Scenarios: A Prelude to Resilience:** Stress testing is a prelude to resilience in making informed adjustments. Investors simulate various scenarios to evaluate how their portfolios would fare under adverse conditions. This proactive approach ensures that the financial composition can withstand unexpected challenges and market turbulence.
- **Cultivating a Resilient Portfolio:** The goal of stress testing is to cultivate a resilient portfolio. Investors identify potential vulnerabilities, adjust risk exposures, and fine-tune the composition to enhance the portfolio's ability to weather storms. This symphony of risk management ensures a well-prepared financial composition.

2. Emergency Funds: The Financial Safety Net Symphony Revisited

- **Linking Informed Adjustments to Emergency Preparedness:** Informed adjustments and emergency funds form a collaborative symphony in financial safety. Linking adjustments to emergency preparedness involves recognizing that unforeseen events can impact both the portfolio and overall financial stability. Maintaining emergency funds ensures a safety net during turbulent market periods.
- **Preserving Financial Stability:** The goal is to preserve financial stability during unforeseen events. Informed adjustments, when integrated into a comprehensive risk management strategy, act as a buffer, allowing investors to weather storms without compromising long-term financial goals.

Market Conditions and Investor Psychology: The Human Tempo in Adjustment Strategies

1. Navigating Market Volatility: A Symphony of Resilience

- **Embracing the Rhythm of Market Fluctuations:** Navigating market volatility is a symphony of resilience. Investors acknowledge that market fluctuations are part of the rhythm in the financial landscape. Making informed adjustments involves embracing this rhythm, and understanding that short-term market movements should not overshadow long-term investment goals.

- **Emotional Fortitude:** Developing emotional fortitude becomes crucial during times of market uncertainty. Investors must resist impulsive decisions driven by short-term market movements and maintain a focus on long-term objectives. Emotional fortitude ensures a steady tempo in the face of market fluctuations.

2. Life Changes: Adapting the Melody to New Chapters

- *Adjusting Portfolios with Life Transitions:* Life changes prompt investors to adapt the melody of their adjustment strategy. Whether entering retirement, facing health challenges, or experiencing a major life event, individuals adjust their portfolios to align with new chapters. Flexibility and a willingness to recalibrate adjustment approaches contribute to a resilient and comprehensive financial plan.

Chapter Eight: Investing for Specific Goals

Education savings

The pursuit of education is a transformative journey, shaping the future of individuals and societies alike. Recognizing the profound impact of education, the importance of thoughtful and humanized approaches to education savings cannot be overstated.

The Human Element: Motivations and Emotional Landscape

1. Motivations Behind Education Savings: Investing in Future Potential

- **Aspiring for Bright Futures:** Education savings are motivated by the deep-seated aspiration for bright futures. Parents, guardians, and individuals aspire to provide the best possible educational opportunities for their loved ones. The emotional landscape involves a commitment to nurturing the potential within each learner, fostering growth, and opening doors to opportunities.

- **Empowering Through Knowledge:** The motivation extends beyond financial considerations to the empowerment derived from knowledge. Education is seen as a powerful tool that empowers individuals to navigate the complexities of life, contribute meaningfully to society, and pursue their passions. Education savings embody the belief in the transformative power of learning.

2. Emotional Nuances of Education Savings: Balancing Sacrifice and Reward

- **Sacrifices for Future Triumphs:** Education savings often entail sacrifices in the present for future triumphs. The emotional nuances include parents and guardians making financial sacrifices, prioritizing education over immediate desires, and recognizing the long-term impact of investing in learning.
- **Anticipation of Future Achievements:** The emotional landscape involves the anticipation of future achievements. Education savings represent not only a financial commitment but an emotional investment in the aspirations and potential accomplishments of the learners. The joy derived from envisioning their educational milestones becomes a driving force in the journey of education savings.

Understanding Education Savings: A Symphony of Financial Insight

1. Starting Early: The Prelude to Financial Preparedness

- **The Power of Compound Growth:** Starting early is the prelude to financial preparedness in education savings. The power of compound growth becomes a vital instrument in this symphony. Early contributions have the potential to grow substantially over time, easing the financial burden when education expenses arise. Parents and guardians act as conductors, orchestrating a melody of foresight and preparation.
- **Setting Realistic Goals:** The journey involves setting realistic goals. Education savings plans must align with the anticipated costs of education, factoring in variables such as inflation and the chosen educational path. Realistic goals provide a clear roadmap for the financial journey, ensuring

that the melody of education savings harmonizes with future needs.

2. *Choosing the Right Savings Instruments: Crafting a Melody of Security*

- *529 Plans: A Harmonious Ensemble:* 529 plans emerge as a harmonious ensemble in education savings. These tax-advantaged savings plans are designed specifically for education expenses. Offering flexibility and potential tax benefits, 529 plans allow individuals to invest in a diverse range of portfolios, providing a comprehensive approach to funding education.
- *Custodial Accounts: Nurturing Financial Growth:* Custodial accounts contribute to the melody by nurturing financial growth. These accounts, such as Uniform Gift to Minors Act (UGMA) or Uniform Transfer to Minors Act (UTMA) accounts, allow assets to be held for the benefit of a minor. While providing flexibility, they come with fewer restrictions on how funds are used for education.

Financial Strategies: Balancing the Symphony of Budget and Investment

1. *Creating a Budget: The Rhythmic Foundation*

- *Aligning Income and Expenses:* Creating a budget forms the rhythmic foundation of education savings. Individuals and families align income and expenses, allocating a portion towards education savings. This strategic budgeting ensures a disciplined approach, harmonizing daily financial decisions with long-term educational aspirations.
- *Emergency Funds: The Safety Net Symphony:* Education savings are interwoven with the safety net symphony of emergency funds. Maintaining a financial safety net ensures that unexpected challenges do not derail education savings plans. The goal is to preserve the harmony of education savings even during unforeseen financial events.

2. Investing Wisely: Orchestrating Growth with Prudence

- *Diversification: A Synchronized Ballet:* Investing wisely involves a synchronized ballet of diversification. Education savings benefit from a diversified portfolio that spreads risk across various asset classes. While seeking growth, diversification acts as a protective measure, ensuring that the melody of education savings is not overly susceptible to market fluctuations.

- *Periodic Reviews: Fine-Tuning the Composition:* Conductors of education savings engage in periodic reviews. Fine-tuning the composition of the investment portfolio involves assessing performance, adjusting asset allocation as needed, and ensuring that the chosen investment instruments align with the goals of education savings. This process ensures the continued harmony of the financial composition.

Risk Management: Safeguarding Melodies in Education Savings

1. Risk Tolerance: The Conductor's Baton in Financial Harmony

- *Aligning with Risk Preferences:* Risk tolerance becomes the conductor's baton in education savings. Individuals must align their education savings strategies with their risk preferences. The goal is to strike a balance that offers growth opportunities while safeguarding against potential market volatility. The conductor navigates the tempo, ensuring that the melody remains harmonious.

- *Flexibility in Risk Management:* The orchestration involves flexibility in risk management. Education savings plans should be adaptable to evolving market conditions and changing risk profiles. This flexibility ensures that education savings remain aligned with the dynamic nature of financial landscapes.

2. Life Changes: Adapting the Melody to New Chapters

- *Adjusting Plans with Educational Transitions:* Life changes prompt adjustments to the melody of education savings. As learners progress through different educational stages, from primary to secondary to higher education, plans must adapt accordingly. Flexibility in education savings allows for adjustments based on changing educational needs and aspirations.
- *Financial Advisors as Conductors:* Financial advisors serve as conductors, guiding individuals through the transitions in education savings. Their expertise helps recalibrate strategies in response to changing circumstances, ensuring that the financial composition remains harmonious.

Homeownership

Homeownership is more than a financial transaction; it's a profound and deeply human experience. It represents a chapter of life where dreams are built, memories are forged, and a sense of belonging takes root.

The Human Element: Motivations and Emotional Landscape

1. Motivations Behind Homeownership: Building a Foundation for Life

- *The Desire for Stability:* Homeownership is often motivated by the desire for stability. Individuals and families seek a place to call their own, a sanctuary where they can plant roots and weather the storms of life. The emotional landscape involves a yearning for a stable foundation upon which to build a fulfilling life.
- *Fulfilling the Dream of Ownership:* The dream of homeownership is deeply embedded in the cultural narrative. It represents a milestone of achievement, a tangible manifestation of hard work and dedication. The emotional nuances include the fulfillment of a dream that goes beyond mere property ownership – it's about crafting a haven that mirrors one's

identity and aspirations.

2. Emotional Nuances of Homeownership: Balancing Aspiration and Practicality

- *Aspirations for a Home:* Homeownership embodies aspirations for a space that reflects personal identity and values. The emotional nuances include envisioning a home as more than just a physical structure; it's a canvas where memories will be painted, relationships will be nurtured, and a lifetime of experiences will unfold.
- *Balancing Practical Considerations:* Amidst the dreams, homeownership involves practical considerations. Emotional nuances include balancing aspirations with financial prudence, understanding the responsibilities that come with owning a home, and ensuring that the journey aligns with both present desires and future needs.

Understanding Homeownership: A Symphony of Financial Insight

1. Financial Preparedness: The Overture to Homeownership

- *Building a Financial Foundation:* Financial preparedness is the overture to homeownership. It involves building a solid financial foundation, assessing creditworthiness, and saving for a down payment. The journey begins with a conductor, orchestrating the initial steps toward turning the dream of homeownership into a tangible reality.
- *Navigating Mortgage Options:* As the symphony unfolds, understanding mortgage options becomes crucial. Homebuyers explore various mortgage structures, interest rates, and terms to find a harmonious arrangement that aligns with their financial capabilities and long-term goals.

2. Choosing the Right Home: Crafting a Melody of Comfort and Aspiration

- *Defining Home Preferences:* Choosing the right home is a melody of comfort and aspiration. It involves defining preferences from location and size to architectural style and amenities. The conductor, in this case, is the individual or family envisioning a harmonious blend of practicality and dream fulfillment.

· **Budgeting Wisely:** The financial composition includes budgeting wisely. Homebuyers carefully evaluate their budget constraints, factoring in not just the purchase price but also ongoing expenses like property taxes, insurance, and maintenance costs. This financial symphony ensures that the chosen home aligns with both lifestyle aspirations and financial prudence.

Financial Strategies: Harmonizing Budget and Investment

1. Creating a Budget: The Rhythmic Foundation

· **Aligning Income and Expenses:** Creating a budget forms the rhythmic foundation of homeownership. Individuals and families align income and expenses, allocating funds not only for mortgage payments but also for ongoing homeownership costs. This strategic budgeting ensures a harmonious relationship between financial stability and homeownership aspirations.

· **Emergency Funds: The Safety Net Symphony:** The safety net symphony involves maintaining emergency funds. Homeownership comes with un-expected repairs and expenses. Having a financial safety net ensures that homeowners can navigate unforeseen challenges without compromising the joy and stability associated with owning a home.

2. Investing Wisely: Orchestrating Growth with Prudence

· **Home Equity as an Asset:** Investing wisely in homeownership includes recognizing home equity as an asset. Homeowners build equity as they pay down their mortgages and as property values appreciate. This asset can serve as a source of financial stability and, in some cases, a resource for future investments.

· **Strategic Renovations and Improvements:** Orchestrating growth involves strategic renovations and improvements. Homeowners may enhance the value of their property through thoughtful upgrades, not only for personal enjoyment but also as a strategic investment. The financial symphony includes balancing improvements that contribute to both present comfort and future resale value

Risk Management: Safeguarding Melodies in Homeownership

1. Home Insurance: The Conductor's Baton in Financial Harmony

· **Protecting Against Unforeseen Events:** Home insurance becomes the conductor's baton in financial harmony. It protects homeowners against unforeseen events such as fire, natural disasters, or theft. Safeguarding the melody of homeownership involves choosing the right insurance coverage to ensure financial resilience in the face of unexpected challenges.
· **Regular Policy Reviews:** *Adapting to Changing Needs:* The symphony requires periodic reviews of insurance policies. As life evolves and property values change, homeowners must adapt their coverage to align with current needs. This proactive approach ensures that the financial composition remains harmonious and adequately protected.

2. Market Conditions and Homeownership: The Human Tempo in Investment Strategies

· **Navigating Real Estate Trends: A Symphony of Adaptability:** Navigating real estate trends is a symphony of adaptability. Homeowners and prospective buyers must recognize the impact of market conditions on their investment. Whether in a buyer's or seller's market, understanding the tempo of real estate trends guides decisions about buying, selling, or refinancing a home.
· **Long-Term Vision:** *The Human Tempo in Investment Strategies:* The human

tempo involves maintaining a long-term vision. Market fluctuations may occur, but homeownership is a long-term investment. The conductor of this symphony recognizes that short-term market movements should not overshadow the enduring value and stability that homeownership brings.

Life Changes: Adapting the Melody to New Chapters

1. Homeownership and Life Transitions: A Symphony of Adaptation

- **Adjusting Homeownership with Life Changes:** Life changes prompt home-owners to adopt the melody of homeownership. Whether it's a growing family, a career move, or retirement, individuals adjust their homes to align with new chapters. Flexibility and a willingness to recalibrate homeownership strategies contribute to a resilient and comprehensive financial plan.
- **Aging in Place: Adapting Homes for the Future:** Aging in place involves adapting homes for the future. As homeowners age, they may modify their residences to enhance accessibility and accommodate changing needs. The financial symphony includes considering renovations that support aging in place, ensuring that homes remain both comfortable and practical.

10

Chapter Nine: Tax Considerations

Tax-efficient investing

T ax-efficient investing is more than a financial strategy; it's a symphony of harmony between wealth accumulation, tax optimization, and individual financial goals.

The Human Element: Motivations and Emotional Landscape

1. Motivations Behind Tax-Efficient Investing: Nurturing Financial Well-Being

- **The Desire for Wealth Preservation:** Tax-efficient investing is often motivated by the desire for wealth preservation. Investors seek strategies that not only generate returns but also minimize the impact of taxes on their hard-earned gains. The emotional landscape involves a commitment to nurturing financial well-being and maximizing the potential for long-term growth.
- **Fulfilling Future Aspirations:** Beyond the numerical aspects, tax-efficient investing embodies the fulfillment of future aspirations. Whether it's saving for a home, funding education, or securing a comfortable retirement, the emotional nuances include a commitment to optimizing tax strategies

in alignment with these cherished life goals.

2. *Emotional Nuances of Tax-Efficient Investing: Balancing Prudence and Aspiration*

- *Prudence in Financial Decision-Making:* Tax-efficient investing requires prudence in financial decision-making. Investors navigate the emotional nuances of balancing the pursuit of returns with the need to minimize tax liabilities. The art lies in making informed choices that harmonize both aspects, ensuring that financial goals are achieved without undue tax burdens.
- *Aspiration for Financial Freedom:* The emotional landscape involves an aspiration for financial freedom. Tax-efficient investing becomes a means to empower individuals to achieve their financial objectives without being encumbered by avoidable tax implications. The emotional nuances include a commitment to crafting a financial journey that aligns with personal aspirations.

Understanding Tax-Efficient Investing: A Symphony of Financial Insight

1 .*Starting Early: The Prelude to Tax Efficiency*

- *The Power of Compounding in a Tax-Advantaged Environment:* Starting early is the prelude to tax efficiency. Investors harness the power of compounding within tax-advantaged environments such as Individual Retirement Accounts (IRAs) or employer-sponsored retirement plans. This early symphony lays the groundwork for tax-efficient wealth accumulation, offering the potential for compounded growth over time.
- *Strategic Asset Location: Crafting a Melody of Tax Efficiency:* The journey involves strategic asset location. Investors allocate assets across taxable and tax-advantaged accounts, aiming to optimize tax efficiency. The melody is crafted by balancing investments based on their tax treatment,

ensuring that tax consequences are minimized while maximizing overall returns.

2. *Choosing Tax-Efficient Investment Vehicles: Crafting a Harmonious Ensemble*

- *Utilizing Tax-Efficient Funds:* Tax-efficient investing encompasses the use of tax-efficient funds. These funds are structured to minimize taxable distributions, allowing investors to defer capital gains and reduce annual tax liabilities. The ensemble is crafted by selecting investments that align with individual tax goals, ensuring a harmonious interplay between returns and tax considerations.
- *Tax-Deferred and Tax-Free Accounts: A Harmonious Chorus:* The harmonious chorus includes tax-deferred and tax-free accounts. Investors leverage vehicles like Roth IRAs, where qualified withdrawals are tax-free, and 401(k)s, which offer tax deferral on contributions. The ensemble is orchestrated by strategically using these accounts to optimize tax outcomes in both the short and long term.

Financial Strategies: Balancing the Symphony of Budget and Investment

1. *Creating a Budget: The Rhythmic Foundation*
Creating a Budget: The Rhythmic Foundation

- *Aligning Income and Expenses with Tax Goals:* Creating a budget forms the rhythmic foundation of tax-efficient investing. Individuals align income and expenses with their tax goals, ensuring that investment decisions are integrated into overall financial planning. The symphony involves budgeting with an awareness of the tax implications, allowing for a synchronized approach to wealth accumulation and tax efficiency.
- *Emergency Funds: The Safety Net Symphony:* Tax-efficient investing is interwoven with the safety net symphony of emergency funds. Maintaining a financial safety net ensures that unexpected challenges do not

compromise the tax efficiency of long-term investment strategies. The goal is to preserve the harmony of tax-efficient investing even during unforeseen financial events.

2. *Investing Wisely: Orchestrating Growth with Prudence*

- *Diversification: A Synchronized Ballet:* Investing wisely involves a synchronized ballet of diversification. Tax-efficient portfolios benefit from a diversified approach that spreads risk across various asset classes. The symphony is crafted by balancing growth-oriented and income-generating investments while considering the tax implications of each component.
- *Periodic Reviews: Fine-Tuning the Composition:* Conductors of tax-efficient investing engage in periodic reviews. Fine-tuning the composition of the investment portfolio involves assessing performance, adjusting asset allocation as needed, and ensuring that the chosen investment instruments align with tax efficiency goals. This process ensures the continued harmony of the financial composition.

Risk Management: Safeguarding Melodies in Tax-Efficient Strategies

1. *Tax-Loss Harvesting: The Conductor's Baton in Financial Harmony*

- *Turning Market Volatility into a Melody:* Tax-loss harvesting becomes the conductor's baton in financial harmony. Investors leverage market volatility to their advantage by strategically realizing losses to offset gains. The symphony involves turning market fluctuations into a melody of tax efficiency, allowing investors to optimize their tax positions during periods of volatility.
- *Discipline in Tax-Loss Harvesting:* The symphony requires discipline in tax-loss harvesting. Investors must navigate emotional impulses during market downturns and execute tax-loss harvesting with a strategic mindset.

The goal is to safeguard melodies in tax-efficient strategies, ensuring that short-term market movements do not disrupt the overarching harmony of long-term tax optimization.

2. *Life Changes: Adapting the Melody to New Chapters*

- *Adjusting Tax-Efficient Strategies with Life Transitions:* Life changes prompt adjustments to the melody of tax-efficient investing. Whether it's a career shift, marriage, or retirement, individuals adapt their tax strategies to align with new chapters. The symphony involves flexibility and a willingness to recalibrate tax-efficient approaches based on changing circumstances, ensuring that financial goals remain harmoniously integrated.

Market Conditions and Investor Psychology: The Human Tempo in Tax-Efficient Strategies

1. *Navigating Tax Planning Through Market Fluctuations: A Symphony of Resilience*

- *Embracing the Rhythm of Market Changes:* Navigating tax planning through market fluctuations is a symphony of resilience. Investors acknowledge that market changes are part of the rhythm in the financial landscape. The symphony involves embracing this rhythm, understanding that short-term market movements should not overshadow long-term tax-efficient goals.
- *Emotional Fortitude:* Developing emotional fortitude becomes crucial during times of market uncertainty. Investors must resist impulsive tax decisions driven by short-term market movements and maintain a focus on long-term tax-efficient objectives. Emotional fortitude ensures a steady tempo in the face of market fluctuations.

2. *Life Changes: Adapting the Melody to New Chapters*

- *Adjusting Tax Strategies with Life Transitions:* Life changes prompt investors to adapt the melody of their tax strategies. Whether entering retirement, facing health challenges, or experiencing a major life event, individuals adjust their tax-efficient portfolios to align with new chapters. Flexibility and a willingness to recalibrate tax strategies contribute to a resilient and comprehensive financial plan.

Capital gains and losses

Capital gains and losses are the dynamic currents that flow through the river of financial markets, shaping the landscape of investment journeys.

The Human Element: Motivations and Emotional Landscape

1. *Motivations Behind Capital Gains and Losses: Navigating Financial Tides*

- **The Desire for Wealth Growth:** Capital gains and losses are often motivated by the overarching desire for wealth growth. Investors engage in the intricate dance of financial markets with the hope of seeing their assets appreciate over time. The emotional landscape involves a commitment to navigating the unpredictable tides of the market in pursuit of financial prosperity.
- **Risk and Reward:** The motivations extend beyond mere accumulation; they embrace the inherent duality of risk and reward. Investors knowingly expose their capital to market fluctuations, understanding that the potential for gains comes hand in hand with the possibility of losses. The emotional nuances include the acceptance of this delicate balance in the pursuit of financial objectives

2. *Emotional Nuances of Capital Gains and Losses: Balancing Expectations and*

Realities

- **Celebrating Gains:** Capital gains evoke a sense of celebration. The emotional nuances include the joy and satisfaction derived from seeing investments appreciate. Whether it's the result of strategic decisions, market timing, or simply good fortune, celebrating gains is a human response to the realization of financial success.
- **Navigating Losses:** On the flip side, losses prompt a different set of emotions. Investors navigate the emotional landscape of disappointment, concern, or even frustration when faced with declines in portfolio value. The art lies in acknowledging and managing these emotions, ensuring that they don't overshadow the rational decision-making required in the face of losses.

Understanding Capital Gains and Losses: A Symphony of Financial Insight

1. The Mechanism of Capital Gains: The Crescendo of Wealth Appreciation

- **Realizing Gains through Appreciation:** The mechanism of capital gains involves realizing profits through the appreciation of asset values. Whether through the sale of stocks, real estate, or other investments, investors experience the crescendo of wealth appreciation when the selling price exceeds the purchase price. The symphony involves strategic decision-making to capitalize on favorable market conditions.
- **Long-Term vs. Short-Term Gains: Harmonizing Investment Horizons:** The symphony encompasses the harmonization of long-term and short-term gains. Different tax treatments apply to gains realized over varying time horizons. Investors strategically navigate these distinctions, considering the tax implications while aligning with their overall investment goals.

2. The Dynamics of Capital Losses: The Resilience in Financial Setbacks

- *Acceptance and Learning from Losses:* The dynamics of capital losses involve the acceptance of financial setbacks as inherent elements of investing. Investors embrace the reality that not every investment will yield positive returns. The symphony includes the capacity to learn from losses, using them as opportunities for reflection, adjustment, and growth in financial acumen.

- *Tax-Loss Harvesting: Optimizing Losses for Tax Efficiency:* Within the symphony, investors may engage in tax-loss harvesting as a strategic response to losses. This involves strategically selling investments at a loss to offset capital gains, minimizing the overall tax impact. The harmony lies in optimizing losses to enhance the tax efficiency of the investment portfolio.

Financial Strategies: Balancing the Symphony of Risk and Return

1. Creating a Balanced Portfolio: The Rhythmic Foundation

- *Diversification: The Synchronized Ballet of Risk Management:* Creating a balanced portfolio forms the rhythmic foundation of managing capital gains and losses. Diversification is the synchronized ballet of risk management. Investors strategically allocate their capital across a variety of assets to spread risk, ensuring that the melody of their financial journey is not overly influenced by the performance of any single investment.

- *Risk Tolerance: Aligning with Individual Comfort:* The rhythmic foundation also involves aligning with individual risk tolerance. Investors must navigate their emotional comfort zones, ensuring that the chosen investment strategy harmonizes with their ability to withstand market fluctuations. The symphony involves a careful balance between risk and comfort, allowing for a sustainable and resilient financial composition.

2. Investing Wisely: Orchestrating Growth with Prudence

- *Periodic Reviews: Fine-Tuning the Composition:* Investing wisely requires a symphony of periodic reviews. Fine-tuning the composition of the investment portfolio involves assessing performance, adjusting asset allocation as needed, and ensuring that the chosen investment instruments align with risk and return objectives. The process ensures the continued harmony of the financial composition amidst the ebb and flow of capital gains and losses.

- *Emotional Discipline: Navigating Market Volatility:* The symphony involves emotional discipline in navigating market volatility. Investors acknowledge that market fluctuations are part of the rhythm in the financial landscape. Emotional fortitude ensures a steady tempo, preventing impulsive decisions driven by short-term movements and maintaining a focus on long-term investment goals.

Life Changes: Adapting the Melody to New Chapters

1. *Adjusting Investment Strategies with Life Transitions: A Symphony of Adaptation*

- *Life Events and Portfolio Adjustments:* Life changes prompt investors to adapt the melody of their investment strategies. Whether it's a career shift, marriage, or retirement, individuals adjust their portfolios to align with new chapters. The symphony involves flexibility and a willingness to recalibrate investment approaches based on changing circumstances, ensuring that financial goals remain harmoniously integrated.
- *Financial Advisors as Conductors:* Financial advisors serve as conductors, guiding individuals through the transitions in investment strategies. Their expertise helps recalibrate strategies in response to changing circumstances, ensuring that the financial composition remains harmonious and aligned with evolving life goals.

11

Chapter Ten: Common Mistakes to Avoid

Market timing

Market timing, the endeavor to predict the optimal moments to buy or sell investments, is a captivating yet challenging dance within the financial landscape.

The Human Element: Motivations and Emotional Landscape

1. Motivations Behind Market Timing: Chasing the Elusive Waves of Opportunity

- **The Desire for Maximum Returns:** Market timing often stems from the desire for maximum returns. Investors embark on the journey with the hope of buying low and selling high, capitalizing on market fluctuations to optimize their investment gains. The emotional landscape involves the pursuit of opportunities to enhance wealth and financial well-being.
- **Fear of Loss:** Another motivation is the fear of loss. Investors may attempt to time the market to avoid downturns and minimize potential losses. The emotional nuances include the natural instinct to protect hard-earned capital from market volatility, reflecting a desire for financial security.

2. *Emotional Nuances of Market Timing: Navigating the Tides of Optimism and Anxiety*

- ***Optimism in Bull Markets:*** In bull markets, optimism prevails as investors ride the wave of positive sentiment. The emotional nuances involve the excitement of potential gains and the fear of missing out on lucrative opportunities. Market timing during these periods is often influenced by the desire to participate in the momentum.
- ***Anxiety in Bear Markets:*** Bear markets bring forth anxiety and apprehension. Emotional nuances include the fear of further losses and the urge to exit the market to preserve capital. Market timing during these periods reflects a defensive stance, driven by the emotional need to shield oneself from potential financial setbacks.

Understanding Market Timing: A Symphony of Financial Insight

1. *The Complexity of Market Dynamics: Interpreting Financial Crescendos and Diminuendos*

- ***Economic Indicators and News Flow:*** Market timing involves interpreting economic indicators and the continuous flow of news that impacts financial markets. Investors navigate the symphony of data, seeking signals that may indicate shifts in market sentiment and influence investment decisions.
- ***Technical Analysis and Chart Patterns:*** Technical analysis, akin to reading musical notes on a sheet, is a tool used in market timing. Investors analyze chart patterns and historical price movements to identify trends and potential turning points. The symphony includes the intricate dance of interpreting these visual cues.

2. *Market Timing Strategies: Crafting a Harmonious Ensemble*

- ***Tactical Asset Allocation:*** Tactical asset allocation is a strategy where investors adjust their portfolio allocation based on short-term market conditions. The ensemble involves dynamically shifting investments to capitalize on perceived opportunities or reduce exposure during perceived risks.

· **Swing Trading and Momentum Strategies:** Swing trading and momentum strategies contribute to the harmonious ensemble of market timing. Investors engage in short-term buying or selling based on price trends and momentum, attempting to capture profits during market upswings.

Financial Strategies: Balancing the Symphony of Risk and Return

1. Creating a Balanced Portfolio: The Rhythmic Foundation

· **Diversification:** *A Synchronized Ballet of Risk Management:* Creating a balanced portfolio forms the rhythmic foundation of market timing. Diversification, like a synchronized ballet, ensures that the impact of market timing decisions on the overall portfolio is moderated. The symphony involves strategically allocating assets to spread risk and maintain a resilient investment stance.

2. Investing Wisely: Orchestrating Growth with Prudence

· **Discipline in Execution:** Investing wisely within the realm of market timing requires discipline in execution. The symphony involves adhering to predetermined strategies and avoiding impulsive decisions driven by short-term market movements. Discipline ensures a steady tempo, preventing emotional reactions that may compromise long-term financial goals.

Risk Management: Safeguarding Melodies in Market Timing Strategies

1. The Conductor's Baton: Risk Mitigation and Adaptive Strategies

· **Risk Mitigation through Stop-Loss Orders:** The conductor's baton involves risk mitigation through tools like stop-loss orders. Investors set predetermined price levels at which they will sell an asset to limit potential losses. The symphony includes using these adaptive strategies to safeguard melodies in market timing, preventing significant financial setbacks.

2. Life Changes: Adapting the Melody to New Chapters

· **Adjusting Market Timing Strategies with Life Transitions:** Life changes prompt adjustments to the melody of market timing strategies. Whether it's a career shift, marriage, or retirement, individuals adapt their approaches to align with new chapters. The symphony involves flexibility and a willingness to recalibrate market timing strategies based on changing circumstances, ensuring that financial goals remain harmoniously integrated.

Market Conditions and Investor Psychology: The Human Tempo in Market Timing Strategies

1.Navigating Market Sentiment: A Symphony of Emotional Intelligence

· **Embracing Contrarian Perspectives:** Navigating market sentiment is a symphony of emotional intelligence. Successful market timing involves embracing contrarian perspectives, where investors may act counter to prevailing market sentiment. The symphony includes the ability to assess and understand the emotional currents that influence market behavior.

2. Market Timing and Long-Term Vision: The Human Tempo in Investment

Strategies

- *Balancing Short-Term Tactics with Long-Term Vision:* The human tempo involves balancing short-term market timing tactics with a long-term vision. While market timing strategies may capitalize on short-term opportunities, the symphony recognizes that long-term investment success requires a broader perspective. Investors harmonize the ebb and flow of market timing within the context of enduring financial goals.

Emotional decision-making

Emotional decision-making in the realm of finances is a captivating and complex dance, where the heart and the mind engage in a delicate interplay.

The Human Element: Motivations and the Emotional Landscape

1. *Motivations Behind Emotional Decision-Making: The Heart's Desires*

- *The Urge for Security and Comfort:* Emotional decision-making often stems from a fundamental urge for security and comfort. Investors and individuals seek financial stability, driven by the emotional need for a sense of safety and assurance about their future. The emotional landscape involves a desire to create a financial cushion that buffers against life's uncertainties.
- *Aspirations for Prosperity:* Beyond security, emotional decisions are motivated by aspirations for prosperity. The human element in financial choices is infused with dreams of a better life, whether it's achieving homeownership, funding education, or retiring comfortably. The emotional nuances include the excitement and passion associated with envisioning and striving for financial goals.

2. *Emotional Nuances of Decision-Making: The Symphony of Optimism and Anxiety*

- **Optimism in Positive Times:** During positive economic periods, optimism often permeates decision-making. The emotional nuances include a sense of confidence and positivity, leading to investment choices driven by the belief in continuous growth. Investors may be more inclined to take risks and make decisions based on the prevailing positive sentiment.
- ***Anxiety in Uncertain Times:*** Conversely, in times of economic uncertainty, anxiety becomes a dominant emotional force. Decision-making is marked by caution, fear of potential losses, and a desire to preserve wealth. The symphony involves navigating the ebb and flow of optimism and anxiety, where emotional decisions fluctuate with the tides of economic conditions.

Understanding Emotional Decision-Making: A Symphony of Financial Insight

1. *Cognitive Biases: The Melody of Mental Shortcuts*

- **Loss Aversion:** Loss aversion, a common cognitive bias, plays a prominent role in emotional decision-making. Investors often feel the impact of losses more acutely than gains, leading to decisions driven by a desire to avoid perceived risks. The symphony involves recognizing and mitigating the influence of loss aversion in financial choices.
- ***Overconfidence Bias:*** Overconfidence bias contributes to the symphony by inflating individuals' belief in their ability to predict market movements or make successful investment decisions. Emotional choices influenced by overconfidence can lead to excessive risk-taking. The melody involves acknowledging one's limitations and fostering a balanced perspective.

2. *Behavioral Finance: The Harmony of Psychology and Economics*

- ***The Role of Heuristics:*** Heuristics, mental shortcuts or rules of thumb, shape the harmony of financial decisions. Investors may rely on heuristics such as following the crowd or sticking to familiar investment options. Understanding the influence of heuristics in decision-making is crucial for orchestrating a balanced financial symphony.

· **The Impact of Social Proof:** Social proof, the tendency to follow the actions of others, becomes part of the symphony. Investors may make decisions based on the behavior of their peers or public figures, creating a collective rhythm in the financial landscape. The melody involves recognizing the impact of social proof and making choices aligned with individual financial goals.

Financial Strategies: Balancing the Symphony of Heart and Mind

1. Creating a Financial Plan: The Rhythmic Foundation

· **Aligning with Personal Values:** Creating a financial plan forms the rhythmic foundation of emotional decision-making. The symphony involves aligning financial goals with personal values, ensuring that choices resonate with individual aspirations. A well-crafted plan provides a structured framework that helps individuals harmonize their emotional desires with pragmatic financial strategies.

· **Emergency Funds: The Safety Net Symphony:** The safety net symphony involves establishing emergency funds. Emotional decisions, often driven by the fear of unforeseen events, find a harmonious resolution in maintaining financial safety nets. These funds act as a buffer, allowing individuals to navigate challenges without compromising their long-term financial symphony.

2. Investing Wisely: Orchestrating Growth with Prudence

· **Diversification: A Synchronized Ballet of Risk Management:** Investing wisely requires a synchronized ballet of risk management. Diversification becomes part of the symphony, balancing risk and return. Emotional decisions, influenced by the fear of concentrated losses, find resolution in a diversified portfolio that weaves together different asset classes. The melody involves crafting an investment strategy that aligns with individual risk tolerance and financial goals.

Risk Management: Safeguarding Melodies in Emotional Decision-Making Strategies

1. Setting Realistic Expectations: The Conductor's Baton

- **The Conductor's Role in Managing Expectations:** The conductor's baton involves setting realistic expectations. Emotional decision-making often leads to unrealistic optimism or unwarranted pessimism. The symphony includes the role of financial advisors and mentors as conductors who guide individuals in managing expectations, fostering a pragmatic perspective on financial goals.

2. Life Changes: Adapting the Melody to New Chapters

- *Adapting Financial Strategies to Life Transitions:* Life changes prompt adjustments to the melody of financial strategies. Whether it's a career shift, marriage, or retirement, individuals adapt their financial approaches to align with new chapters. The symphony involves flexibility and a willingness to recalibrate financial decisions based on changing circumstances, ensuring that financial goals remain harmoniously integrated.

Market Conditions and Investor Psychology: The Human Tempo in Financial Choices

Navigating Market Sentiment: A Symphony of Emotional Intelligence

- *Embracing a Balanced Approach in Market Fluctuations:* Navigating market sentiment is a symphony of emotional intelligence. Emotional decision-making often intensifies during market fluctuations. The melody involves embracing a balanced approach, acknowledging the emotional currents that influence market behavior while maintaining a steadfast commitment to long-term financial goals.

- *Resilience in the Face of Uncertainty:* Emotional intelligence in financial decisions includes cultivating resilience. Investors navigate the human tempo by developing the emotional fortitude to withstand market uncertainties. The symphony involves recognizing that emotional decisions, even in challenging times, should be guided by a strategic, long-term vision.

12

Chapter Eleven: Resources and Tools

Recommended books, websites, and apps

E mbarking on the path of financial literacy is a transformative
journey, and the tools we choose play a crucial role in shaping our
understanding of personal finance.

The Human Element: Motivations and the Quest for Financial Knowledge

1. Motivations Behind Seeking Recommended Resources: The Aspiration for Financial Mastery

- *The Hunger for Knowledge:* The pursuit of recommended books, websites, and apps often begins with a hunger for knowledge. Individuals seek to understand the principles of personal finance, driven by a desire to take control of their financial destinies. The emotional landscape involves a sense of curiosity and empowerment that comes with acquiring the tools to make informed financial decisions.
- *Empowerment through Technology:* The integration of technology in financial education is motivated by the aspiration for empowerment. Mod-

ern individuals recognize the role of apps and websites in making financial information accessible and user-friendly. The emotional nuances include a sense of confidence gained through leveraging technological tools for financial management.

2. Emotional Nuances of Exploring Recommended Resources: The Symphony of Curiosity and Trust

- **Curiosity as a Driving Force:** Curiosity becomes a driving force when exploring recommended resources. The emotional nuances include the excitement of learning, discovering new financial perspectives, and understanding practical applications. Individuals embark on this journey with a sense of wonder and a desire to expand their financial horizons.
- **Trust in Authoritative Wisdom:** Trust is interwoven into the emotional symphony, especially when choosing recommended books. Individuals place their trust in renowned authors and experts, relying on their wisdom to guide them through the complexities of personal finance. The emotional landscape involves a sense of security in learning from trusted voices.

Understanding Recommended Books: A Symphony of Timeless Wisdom

1. Classics in Personal Finance: The Melody of Time-Tested Knowledge

- **Rich Dad Poor Dad by Robert Kiyosaki: The Financial Storytelling Overture:** "Rich Dad Poor Dad" serves as a financial storytelling overture, narrating the contrasting financial philosophies of two father figures. The symphony involves the emotional resonance of personal narratives, encouraging readers to rethink their approach to wealth-building and financial education.
- **The Total Money Makeover by Dave Ramsey: The Transformational Crescendo:** "The Total Money Makeover" creates a transformational

crescendo in personal finance literature. The emotional landscape involves a journey of financial renewal, as readers embrace Ramsey's actionable steps to eliminate debt, build an emergency fund, and achieve financial peace.

2. Modern Perspectives: The Harmony of Contemporary Insights

- *Your Money or Your Life by Vicki Robin and Joe Dominguez: The Lifestyle Harmony:* "Your Money or Your Life" contributes to the lifestyle harmony in personal finance literature. The symphony involves a deep dive into the relationship between money and life choices, urging readers to align their spending with their values. The emotional nuances include a sense of liberation gained through mindful financial living.
- *The Millionaire Next Door by Thomas J. Stanley and William D. Danko: The Real-Life Sonata:* "The Millionaire Next Door" plays a real-life sonata, offering insights into the habits and characteristics of everyday millionaires. The emotional landscape involves a shift in perspective, as readers discover that wealth-building is often a result of frugality, discipline, and strategic financial choices.

Understanding Recommended Websites: The Harmonious Ensemble of Digital Wisdom

1. Personal Finance Blogs: A Melody of Practical Insights

- *The Points Guy: Navigating the Travel Symphony:* "The Points Guy" navigates the travel symphony, providing insights into maximizing travel rewards and credit card benefits. The symphony involves a harmonious blend of wanderlust and financial strategy, as readers learn to leverage points and miles for memorable journeys.
- *NerdWallet: The Comprehensive Financial Orchestra:* NerdWallet acts as a comprehensive financial orchestra, offering tools and advice on various aspects of personal finance. The emotional landscape involves a sense of

guidance and reliability, as users access resources to compare financial products, budget effectively, and make informed decisions.

2. Investment Platforms: The Rhythmic Foundation of Wealth Growth

- **Investopedia: The Educational Rhythm:** Investopedia sets the educational rhythm, providing in-depth articles and tutorials on a wide range of financial topics. The symphony involves a continuous learning experience, as users deepen their understanding of investment strategies, market trends, and economic principles.
- **Morningstar: The Investment Serenade:** Morningstar contributes to the investment serenade, offering comprehensive insights into investment products, mutual funds, and market analysis. The emotional nuances include a sense of serenity as users access data to make informed investment decisions aligned with their financial goals.

Understanding Recommended Apps: The Symphony of Technological Convenience

1. Budgeting Apps: Orchestrating Financial Harmony on the Go

- **Mint: The Harmonious Budgeting Ensemble:** Mint orchestrates a harmonious budgeting ensemble, providing users with a comprehensive view of their financial landscape. The symphony involves a user-friendly experience, as individuals track expenses, set financial goals, and receive personalized insights to manage their money effectively.
- **YNAB (You Need A Budget): The Empowerment Anthem:** YNAB serves as the empowerment anthem, guiding users to allocate every dollar with intention. The emotional landscape involves a sense of control and empowerment as individuals adopt a proactive approach to budgeting, breaking the paycheck-to-paycheck cycle.

2. Investment Apps: The Melody of Accessible Wealth Building

- *Robinhood: The Inclusive Investment Sonata:* Robinhood plays the inclusive investment sonata, democratizing access to the stock market for users of all backgrounds. The symphony involves a sense of financial inclusion and empowerment, as individuals engage in commission-free trading and explore investment opportunities.
- *Acorns: The Micro-Investment Lullaby:* Acorns contributes to the micro-investment lullaby, allowing users to invest spare change automatically. The emotional nuances include a gentle introduction to investing, fostering a sense of financial progress through small, consistent contributions.

Life Changes: Adapting the Melody to New Chapters

- *Tools for Major Life Events:* Tools for major life events facilitate a symphony of adaptation. Individuals use resources to navigate financial planning for events such as marriage, childbirth, or career changes. The melody involves flexibility and a willingness to recalibrate financial strategies based on changing circumstances, ensuring financial goals remain harmoniously integrated.
- *Financial Advisors as Conductors:* Financial advisors serve as conductors, guiding individuals through the transitions in financial strategies. Their expertise helps recalibrate approaches in response to changing circumstances, ensuring that the financial composition remains harmonious and aligned with evolving life goals.

Investment calculators

In the intricate landscape of personal finance, investment calculators stand out as powerful tools that illuminate the path to financial prosperity.

The Human Element: Motivations and the Desire for Financial Clarity

1. Motivations Behind Using Investment Calculators: The Quest for Financial Confidence

- **The Need for Clarity:** The utilization of investment calculators often arises from the need for financial clarity. Individuals embark on a journey to understand the potential outcomes of their investment decisions, seeking a clearer picture of how their money can grow over time. The emotional landscape involves a desire for confidence, and aligning investments with personal goals and aspirations.
- **Empowerment through Insight:** Beyond clarity, the use of investment calculators is driven by the aspiration for empowerment. Individuals recognize that financial decisions carry long-term consequences, and the emotional nuances include a sense of control gained through insights into how different factors impact their investment portfolios.

2. Emotional Nuances of Using Investment Calculators: The Symphony of Anticipation and Planning

- **Anticipation of Future Wealth:** Anticipation becomes a dominant emotion when using investment calculators. The emotional nuances involve excitement and optimism as individuals project into the future, envisioning the potential growth of their investments. The symphony is one of hope and anticipation, as users explore the possibilities that disciplined investing can unlock.
- **Strategic Planning for Financial Goals:** Strategic planning is interwoven into the emotional symphony, especially when using calculators for specific financial goals. Individuals engage in a thoughtful and strategic process, aligning their investment strategies with milestones such as buying a home, funding education, or achieving a comfortable retirement. The emotional landscape involves a sense of purpose and direction in

financial planning

Understanding Investment Calculators: A Symphony of Financial Insight

1. Retirement Planning Calculators: The Crescendo of Future Financial Well-Being

- **Forecasting Retirement Needs:** Retirement planning calculators create a crescendo of future financial well-being. Users input various parameters, such as current savings, expected retirement age, and desired lifestyle, to estimate the amount needed for a comfortable retirement. The symphony involves a forward-looking perspective, harmonizing dreams of a worry-free retirement with the practicalities of financial preparation.
- **Scenario Planning: The Adaptive Symphony:** The adaptive symphony includes scenario planning tools within retirement calculators. Individuals explore different financial scenarios, preparing for unexpected events and adjusting their retirement strategies accordingly. The emotional landscape involves a sense of resilience gained through proactive planning for various life circumstances.

2. Risk Tolerance Calculators: The Harmonious Ensemble of Personalized Investment Strategies

- **Understanding Individual Risk Appetite:** Risk tolerance calculators contribute to the harmonious ensemble of personalized investment strategies. Users assess their comfort levels with market fluctuations and potential losses, guiding them toward investment portfolios aligned with their risk appetites. The symphony involves a tailored approach, acknowledging the diversity of investors and their unique emotional responses to risk.
- **Balancing Risk and Reward:** The emotional nuances in risk tolerance calculators include a delicate balance between risk and reward. Individuals navigate the symphony of investment decisions, ensuring that their

portfolios reflect a level of risk that resonates with their financial goals and emotional comfort.

Strategic Investment Calculators: Balancing the Symphony of Growth and Stability

1. Compound Interest Calculators: The Melody of Long-Term Wealth Accumulation

- **Embracing the Power of Compounding:** Compound interest calculators play a melody of long-term wealth accumulation. Users witness the exponential growth of their investments over time, emphasizing the importance of patience and consistent contributions. The symphony involves an appreciation for the power of compounding, fostering a long-term perspective in financial planning.
- **Motivation for Consistent Contributions:** The emotional landscape within compound interest calculators includes motivation for consistent contributions. Users find inspiration in seeing how small, regular investments can lead to significant wealth accumulation. The symphony involves a commitment to disciplined financial habits that align with the rhythms of compound growth.

2. Savings Goal Calculators: The Rhythmic Foundation of Financial Objectives

- **Setting Achievable Financial Milestones:** Savings goal calculators act as the rhythmic foundation in setting achievable financial milestones. Users input specific savings goals, whether for a vacation, an emergency fund, or a major purchase, and the calculator outlines the required contributions over time. The symphony involves a harmonious blend of ambition and practicality, guiding individuals toward tangible financial objectives.
- **Celebrating Milestone Achievements:** The emotional nuances within savings goal calculators include the celebration of milestone achievements.

As users track their progress toward financial objectives, there's a sense of accomplishment and motivation to continue the journey. The symphony involves a rhythm of setting, pursuing, and celebrating financial milestones.

Life Changes: Adapting the Melody to New Chapters

1. Adapting Investment Strategies to Life Transitions: A Symphony of Flexibility

- *Tools for Major Life Events:* Investment calculators become tools for major life events, facilitating a symphony of adaptation. Individuals use resources to navigate changes such as career shifts, marriage, or parenthood, adjusting their investment strategies to align with new chapters. The melody involves flexibility and a willingness to recalibrate financial decisions based on changing circumstances, ensuring that investment goals remain harmoniously integrated.
- *Financial Advisors as Conductors:* Financial advisors serve as conductors, guiding individuals through transitions in investment strategies. Their expertise helps recalibrate approaches in response to changing circumstances, ensuring that the investment composition remains harmonious and aligned with evolving life goals.

13

Conclusion

Summarizing key points

1. *Foundational Importance of Investing:*

- Emphasizes investing as a journey toward securing the future.

2. *Setting Clear Financial Goals:*

- Establishing specific and achievable financial milestones.

3. *Diverse Investment Types:*

- Exploring stocks, bonds, real estate, and more for a well-rounded portfolio.

4. *Managing Risk and Return:*

- Balancing risk and return for optimized investment outcomes.

5. *Practical Financial Strategies:*

- Creating budgets, building emergency funds, and differentiating short-term and long-term goals.

6. Retirement Planning:

- Highlighting the significance of strategic retirement planning.

7. Proactive and Empowered Mindset:

- Encouraging continuous learning, adaptability, and leveraging technology.

8. Humanized Approach:

- Acknowledging the emotional aspects, motivations, and resilience in financial decision-making.

Encouraging a proactive approach to investing

1. A Empowering the Conductor Within:

At the heart of this journey is the recognition that you are the conductor of your financial symphony. Each decision, each investment, and each calculated risk is a note that contributes to the masterpiece of your financial future. The conductor within you possesses the wisdom gained from these pages, and as you stand at the podium of your financial life, may you feel a newfound sense of authority and confidence.

2. A Melody of Continuous Learning:

The symphony doesn't end; it evolves. The commitment to continuous learning, illustrated throughout this book, is your melody of growth. Embrace curiosity, stay informed, and let the pursuit of knowledge be a perpetual source of inspiration. Your financial journey is a dynamic composition, and as you adapt and learn, the melody becomes richer, more nuanced, and uniquely yours.

3. Harmony in Setting Goals:

Setting clear financial goals is the harmonic foundation of your symphony. With each goal achieved, may you find not just success but a profound sense of purpose. Let the milestones you reach be the high notes that resonate in your financial memory, motivating you to compose even loftier aspirations. The melody of purpose-driven financial goals is the heartbeat of a fulfilling financial life.

4. The Resilience of Adaptability:

As you navigate the unpredictable rhythms of the financial markets, remember the resilience woven into the fabric of a proactive approach. Adaptability is your ally, and every adjustment to your portfolio is a testament to your ability to weather the storms and seize the opportunities. May your symphony echo with the resilience born from experience and the wisdom to dance with market fluctuations.

5. Instruments of Technology and Tools:

In the modern financial orchestra, technology and tools are your instruments of efficiency and precision. Embrace them with confidence, letting them amplify your financial acumen. The symphony of financial success is harmonized with the efficiency of informed choices made possible by the digital instruments at your disposal.

6. Legacy in Every Note:

As you close this chapter, envision the legacy you are creating. Your financial symphony is not only for you but for the generations that follow. Each note is a legacy of wisdom, discipline, and empowerment. May your financial journey inspire those who come after you to compose their own symphonies of abundance, security, and purpose.

www.ingramcontent.com/pod-product-compliance
Lightning Source LLC
Chambersburg PA
CBHW071047290526
45795CB00004B/1358